CHAPTER 1

The Final Frontier

"I wore a fifty-pound emotional jacket... I was able to enjoy my personal joy and sleep well because of the jacket's high price. I began to shed the jacket and regain all of my power.

Lisa Nichols -- Lisa Nichols She is the woman in self-help section of the bookstore. Always looking for answers. She sits in the back row of personal development courses. She takes notes, has epiphanies, and tries to get better. She has done so much work and made so much progress. Yet, she is still stuck in a body that she hates, ignores and resents. She feels heavy in her body. It feels like she is carrying more than just her body weight. She also carries the weight of unresolved losses, unexpressed hurts, and a lifetime of emotional pain. She feels as if she would rather not be seen. Why? How could it be good to be seen? Attention feels unsafe. It can feel unsafe sometimes.

This woman was me. Perhaps she is also you. I was able to do so much spiritual and emotional work, but still kept my body armor on. It was a great self-protection tactic. I see it all the time in many women. They are happy and successful, but are using denial or avoidance of unreleased weight as a protection mechanism. They are unable to connect with the real person underneath all of this. They compensate for the lack of consciousness by utilizing their gifts and abilities in caring for others, supporting, nurturing, and taking care of them. The final frontier for them is the loss of their weight and the reasons they have this body armor.

It is possible to remain stuck in fearful areas even if you've done a lot of personal development work. It is important to not judge yourself or admonish others. You may have focused on your emotional healing, but neglected your body. Could that be true? It's true. I was deeply involved in healing the emotional aspects of my trauma. I processed too much, or so I thought. But, later, I realized that I was obsessing about overthinking, worrying and obsessing. Because I was addicted to suffering, I felt comfortable in this space. This is very different from feeling your emotions. Although I had high levels of perception, and a deep knowledge of many philosophies; however, they didn't have any grounding in me. They were too difficult to live. Spirituality and emotional work were my comfort zones. I used them to disconnect from my body and mind.

The body aspect was even more apparent: I was unable to eat properly, did not exercise regularly, wore clothing that was comfortable, was sexy, and felt disconnected from almost all aspects of my life.

It was more difficult with the mind. I found myself too smart for my own good. This is what you might find troubling. Although I was intuitive, emotional, and empathic, I let my ego run the show. Everything was my obsession. I was constantly worried about what other people thought of my personality. I was unable to control the future and I worried about it. I thought about all the things that had happened in my past. I couldn't see that my lifelong habit of choosing drama and suffering over seeing the truth was that I had made a choice to choose pain and suffering. As a result, I was left with a lot of unprocessed emotions that I hadn't fully felt or allowed myself to heal. They were all I believed I was processing, but I didn't know that I was actually bypassing them.

This is a common factor for all humankind. However, I have observed a fascinating phenomenon: Women, especially sensitive and intelligent women, often use their intelligence, sensibility, and awareness to avoid healing themselves. Crazy, isn't it? Many women are spiritual seekers and high achievers. They have many years of experience, but still have to lose the excess weight. This doesn't necessarily mean that you did anything wrong or didn't achieve something you wanted. This simply means you are focusing on the areas that are most comfortable and ignoring others. Many people believe that the weight they haven't shed is their blind spot. Subconsciously, we end up hypnotizing our true desires.

Survival Mode

Even though it may not be healthy, the feeling of safety we get from traumatic experiences can be very effective. As I learned to numb and disconnect with my body, or even from having one, we can learn to disassociate ourselves from it. Our nervous system only has one priority: to keep us safe. Congratulations if you were able to create layers of fat!

The alternative was too painful and your younger self wouldn't be able to cope emotionally. She might not have made it through school or suffered a mental breakdown. Or she may have hurt herself more emotionally or physically.

Although it may sound dramatic, this was actually a survival mechanism. Most likely, you didn't have the tools to deal with your emotions. You can only imagine what it was like as a child, because most adults don't know how to deal with trauma and emotions.

Gaining weight is a smart decision because our bodies are our natural protection. Your body is your defense against physical attack. Our brain's reptilian portion reacts instinctively to danger. This is sometimes called our freeze-flight, fight mode. Our emotional bodies are able to protect us as well. It is not hard to believe how many women have suffered trauma from sexual, physical, emotional, or cultural abuse.

Look at the statistics! One in five women has been raped in her lifetime, and these are only the numbers reported! My rapes were not reported by me, nor have many, many others. My personal experience shows that I gained weight immediately after my first rape. You will learn more about this in the next chapter. Although I wasn't aware of what was happening, it was clear from my childhood photos and my psyche that I was trying to protect my self by gaining weight.

Trauma can take many forms, including sexual, physical and emotional abuse. There are also other types of trauma that aren't as obvious but can cause deep wounds. Although cultural expectations and judgments can have the same traumatizing effect on us, they are subtler and travel under the culture.

White privilege and patriarchy, for example, have created generations of shameful self-judgments and internalized self-judgments that affect women's relationships with their bodies. Women are conditioned to believe that a thinner, lighter-skinned body is desirable. If you don't have it, you won't be as beautiful, sensual, and attractive as those with it. This message is conveyed in many ways, including media and films. It becomes even more traumatizing when you consider living in a body that was historically seen as less than human or at bottom of the barrel. All people of color, women of color, trans and queer people, and people with disabilities have learned early on that society doesn't consider them to be equals. In return, they often internalize these messages and develop self-hatred. As a queer, first-generation Chinese American, this is exactly what happened to me. I then tried to make myself into someone else because I hated myself.

The unconscious mind is strong and will protect us from any harm. Our unconscious minds make protection our number one priority.

Using our weight as a shield is actually a great method of protecting ourselves. Camouflage is a common defense tactic used by both animals and armies. The same thing can be done by humans with more weight.

Hiding

Most people associate hiding with feeling unsafe. Fear of being seen on the streets, being visible and promoting your business via social media, or being afraid to let a potential partner or lover into your most intimate and vulnerable spaces. This is a common occurrence and it was certainly the case for me.

The truth is, however, that any perception we have of the outside world is only a projection from our inner world.

I was unable to see the true me because of my weight. There was always a part of me that I wanted to let out. But I couldn't access it and it felt safer not to. It was a fear that I would meet the woman behind my fear fat suits, a woman who was powerful, confident and free. She was also incredibly connectable. I figured that if I lost the emotional and physical weight it would mean that I was "forced" into creating the life I wanted. I would have to accept new and difficult roles that I didn't trust and that I couldn't sustain. Or worse, I might lose the weight that I had once achieved.

My biggest fear is not having what I want in my life. It is impossible to have what you want. To avoid rejection and loss, it's safer to be comfortable than to move away from true and lasting change and transformation.

Martyrdom & Boundaries

A second possible outcome of trauma can be confusion about boundaries. It is possible to not know how healthy boundaries should be established or how to relate to others. We may believe that our bodies aren't ours and therefore not worthy or valuable if they have been breached. Some women use a weight buffer to protect themselves from this. We find another way to say "no" through our bodies, since we are unable to connect to our power or use our voice during fearful and vulnerable situations. It is possible to make ourselves less attractive and avoid being sexually abused again. Perhaps we can gain weight and disappear into the background. Our parents, teachers, and other important people in our lives will not abuse us as they won't see us. We will be invisible.

We learn to prioritize the needs of others and focus on their needs rather than our own. We often try to find meaning in our lives by fixing, caringtaking, and pleasing others. This is because we lack self-esteem. While you may believe you're a good person because of all the good things you've done, the truth is you're using your tendency to focus on others to escape from yourself. This is a common and brilliant tactic. It can boost your self-esteem and give you a false sense worth. But in reality it's a band-aid and a weak one.

After my rapes, all that I had would be given away. This could include my money, time, attention, energy or caretaking. Since my body had been treated in that manner, I felt like disposable trash so I behaved accordingly. I behaved as though my life was not mine. You wouldn't have believed I was doing what I did because of how hard I worked to make myself a fiery, outspoken woman. Behind this façade, I was afraid of real connection. I was afraid of real connection. This mask kept me from feeling truly lacking.

Do you feel the need to rescue, fix, or save someone or something? Although it may appear that you're trying to do good, and you may believe you mean well, the truth is you are actually chasing a distorted version of control because your inner self is so out of control. Because you are the one who truly wants to save others, it is possible to feel the need to help them. Helping others may give you a sense of self-worth, which can be a way to find your intrinsic worthiness. It is possible to feel like you are responsible for the suffering and well-being of others. Your behavior may be that of a martyr if you feel this way. It is difficult because while you may believe you are doing good from the kindness of your heart and are giving back, underneath all that, you are looking for love and a sense worth it. It is possible that you are not giving from a place where you feel fullness and self-love. Instead, you give to get.

Self-Sabotage

Are you happy in the skin that you are in?

Are you happy with what you see in your mirror?

Do you ever look in the mirror at yourself?

Are you influenced by what society considers beautiful or do you define beauty for yourself?

Many women I have spoken to admit that they have tried so many times to lose weight that they no longer trust themselves. Fear of failure keeps them trapped in a vicious cycle of feeling "not good enough" and feeling completely powerless to lose the extra weight that they've been hiding behind. Do you relate? Are you able to relate?

You will most likely feel unhappy and unfulfilled if you keep your weight down, even if everything else is going well. There's probably a nagging feeling inside that you feel empty. This is because you resist taking care of yourself and letting go of the weight. Even though you're a happy person by most standards, there is a part of yourself that feels dead inside. I wanted to feel more than just happy. I wanted to feel alive! I wanted to feel energized and juicier. I was looking for something more than mediocre. I wanted to live the best life possible.

You're probably reading this book to get rid of certain aspects of yourself. You may be telling yourself in secret that you cannot have everything you want, because it is more difficult than you think. Self-sabotage is a common form of self-destructive behavior. When you subconsciously agree to keep yourself in your comfort zone, you can make self-sabotage happen. Your subconscious mind will find a way to return you to your familiar territory when you reach a certain level. You may have self-sabotaged shortly after you achieve success in a particular area or get something you want. Self-sabotage can happen in almost any way you can imagine. Here are some examples:

- You finally scored a meeting with the CEO, and then you get extremely ill and can't make it.
- You fall madly in love with someone, and as soon as they talk about marriage, you create a huge fight and then break up (this was my brilliant way of sabotaging relationships).
- You start to release the weight and feel good in your body and then start overeating again and gain all the weight back plus an extra few pounds.

Gay Hendricks' book "The Big Leap", which explains unconscious sabotage, is a great resource. It is described as "upper-limiting", and it is truly eye-opening.

The Possibilities

Congratulations if any or all of these chapters resonated with your feelings. You are a master saboteur. You are now ready to choose the next phase in your life.

The new way of living does not require hiding. Living a fully embodied life is the new way to live. It's about being connected to your highest self as well as to others. It's about feeling sensual, sexy and confident in your body. It's about radiating a cultivated 'turn-on' out into the world through your job, your relationships, and your very essence while you walk down the street, or looking in the mirror.

It is one thing to be in alignment in a few areas of your life. But it is quite another to be in all areas. Everything clicks when all three realms are given the love and attention they deserve. You are self-realizing and there is no stopping you. When you can feel the power and guidance of the divine, it is easy to realize why you are here. You feel a sense of purpose and clarity, and you feel a deep love and joy inside. You realize that you are living the best life possible and are ready to make quantum leaps towards achieving your greatest dreams. You can still see that vision even if it's "forgotten". Your dreamer is always present in your life, and you can't stop it when you are expressing your true self.

If we are loving and attentive to ourselves, anything is possible. All parts of your body that have been ignored and disconnected for many years are waiting for this moment. You will be able to receive miracles upon miracles by listening to her and committing yourself to loving your body. You will be able to tap into her wisdom and allow her to guide you in the most amazing ways. You will feel more connected to yourself and others when she is calm and content. You will be able to express yourself in the best way possible. Your body is eager to show you the possibilities.

CHAPTER 2

My Fear Fat Suit Story

"We enjoy the beauty of the butterflies, but we rarely acknowledge the sacrifices it has made to attain that beauty."

Maya Angelou's story is about self-forgiveness, and learning to love everyone.

I have dealt with many traumas, which contributed to my fear fat suit, but also my freedom.

Who Am I?

My first trauma experience was when I was caught between two cultures: my Chinese immigrant family, where I felt most secure, and America's culture, where everyone looked and acted the same as me.

Since the day I was five years old, I felt shame at not belonging. At five years of age, I decided to refuse to attend Chinese school. I felt the effects of self-hatred growing within me. This was the beginning of my struggle for identity and longing to be different. My hatred of being Chinese grew as I grew older. It didn't matter that she was valedictorian of the top university in Taiwan and held a master's degree in biochemistry. People treated her like she was less than and I did the same by abandoning my cultural heritage and hers.

Growing up in a predominantly black environment, there was always a part of me that wished I was. I wanted to get away from the shame of being called Asians for all the things they were. My young, naive view was that the black children had it easy because they were the most popular. My life was full of "Ching Chong" or other slurs.

When I was in high school, my name had changed to Stephanie. I didn't like my birth name. I hated myself. Every year, I sneaked into class before the start of each new school year and asked the teacher to call my name Stephanie during roll call. I was disgusted by the way other students called my Pong Ho or Ping Pong. So, I changed my name to Stephanie in an attempt to end this abuse. I had hoped that changing my name would allow me to change how I felt, but it wasn't the case.

When I was in college, my name had changed to Chyna. I wanted to forget my high school traumatizing years and start over. It was also a attempt (albeit a flawed one) to own my Chinese identity. Although "Chyna", was a disguise that allowed me to claim my heritage, it was only one side of the self-hatred coin. Because I was not happy with the way people treated me in highschool, I decided to try something else out of desperation. I didn't realize that I was running from the problem. When I was 25 years old, I went to China as an adult for the first and only time that I began to let go of the shame I felt about being Chinese. I went back to work and asked for people to call me Po. It was a start, and it meant something. After a long, winding road of self-love, my name began to be my love. Years later, I was finally able to call myself Po-Hong.

Lost and Not Found

Since I can remember, my mother was a sensitive and empathic person. As the baby of my family, I felt it was my responsibility ensure that my family felt connected. I saw myself as the center of the wheel, the essential element that held my family together. When my parents divorced at the age of eleven, I felt totally alone, stunned, and sidelined. It was a shock to me that I was thrust into an unfathomable reality. There was no communication or feelings. My parents didn't have a culture where feelings were a normal part of their lives. My parents were loving and supportive, which doesn't mean they didn't love me. This made their divorce a traumatic experience for me.

My family, whom I loved with all my heart, was now broken. I lived now with my mother and Sifu, my new stepfather. My dad moved into a new home. My 16-year-old brother, who I loved and looked up to, moved to another home. All that I loved and knew was gone. It was so overwhelming to feel so scared and alone. I was unable to understand the feelings inside me and didn't know how to communicate them. I remained silent, in pain, and without any support. I felt an empty feeling growing inside me and wanted to fill it. So I did exactly that. I looked in all the wrong places for love, unconsciously.

When I got my first period at age 11, I was about to enter my teens. My hormones and emotions were in full swing. I was looking for the answer to all my prayers. Boys could fill the void and loneliness in my heart, I thought. They paid attention to me and told me what I wanted. I was very shy and naive. I had never heard of sex. I was totally clueless about sex, my body and boys. This left me vulnerable.

Thomas, a 17-year-old boy, approached me one day in the park. His attention, words and affection made me feel special. I was able to forget the loss of my family when he focused on me. He arranged a time to meet me at Mike's house, and informed me that Mike's mother would be there. When we arrived at Mike's house, Thomas said casually, "Oh, his mom isn't home." "She had to do something." Mike brought Thomas and me down to the basement, then left us alone. I felt uneasy and my body wanted to move, but I couldn't. Fear kept me frozen in fear.

Thomas raped me. I was twelve years old, a virgin. There was bleeding, pain and so many other aspects to the experience that shocked and traumatized. I didn't have the maturity nor understanding to deal with any of it. Only I noticed that Thomas seemed happy to have taken my virginity. He viewed it as a badge of honour; now he said he was a real man. He told Mike about it, I'm certain. In shock and confusion, I quickly walked home. I was in shock and confused when I reached my father on the way back. I pretending to be fine. I told my dad that I had my period, and needed to get clean. He laughed at it.

It was at that moment that the seed of shame and self-abandonment was planted. I felt dirty but didn't know why, because I was unaware that I had been subject to rape. I had no idea what rape was and didn't have the word rape in my vocabulary. Thomas did not physically hold me down so I assumed something was wrong. Because I felt bad, I knew this was my fault. This was what I had done. I was terrible.

Even though I didn't know that my innocence had been violated, all the signs and symptoms of a rape victim were present in me. My personality and appearance changed almost like a clockwork. I transformed from being shy to being loud, angry, and rebellious teenager. In a matter of a year, I gained twenty pounds from a healthy weight. To distract myself from my pain, I began hanging out with girls who smoked marijuana and drank alcohol.

When I was thirteen, I had my first drink. Bacardi 151 straight out of the bottle was what it was. It was a sensation of burning in my stomach and throat. I also remember the feeling of calm and peace that overtook me. Numbness felt like heaven. It was so wonderful to finally find something that could numb the pain I'd been experiencing for so many years.

I was already dying in my body so I tried to kill myself outside. When I was thirteen years of age, I attempted suicide by drinking a Tylenol Extra-Strength. I wanted to flee so bad, to no longer exist, to disappear and not feel any more.

I was able to wake up with severe stomach pains in the middle of the night and tell my mom. She brought me to the hospital in panic. I was placed in a halfway house for troubled teens. My roommate had bulimia. I shared a room with many teens who were more troubled than I was. Looking back, I realize that I was the one who needed to be there. I was as sick as any of the children there, and I needed immediate help.

Unfortunately, I wasn't able to get the help I needed because I was embarrassed that my high school students knew I had attempted suicide. My therapist convinced me that I would never try suicide again. I confessed to her that I did it only for attention. This was very true, and, as I now realize, quite insightful. I was in desperate need of help, but didn't know how to get it. I was released from the halfway house with the condition that family therapy would be started. However, I wasn't ready to go and my parents weren't able to handle my emotions. I didn't know who I was. I think that my trauma was so overwhelming that I didn't have the tools or resources to deal with it.

I escalated with rebellious rage, and did what I wanted. I snuck boys in my room, got drunk in the worst parts Boston, while hanging out with gang members, and drove drunk. My mom didn't know what to do. My mom was unsure what to do with me. I used to curse her and act out in the worst ways possible while still working at a bakery and going school. Over the next three years, I spiraled out-of-control and was raped three times more times, including one gang rape. Because I was completely disconnected from my body and my life, I didn't care about my body or my health. An innocent girl was abandoned and a new, bad, 'who cares?' version of me emerged. This was my only hope of surviving the trauma, pain, abuse, and self-hate. I felt like a piece of meat, which was only here to serve other people's needs. So I did what I had to do.

Fear Fat Suit

As a young man, the rapes that I suffered, along with all the other traumas that I had experienced, created deep-seated fear, anger, and shame. It would take me many decades to overcome and heal this shame. The physical manifestation of my emotional pain was manifested in the weight I gained that time. It is now my fear fat suit.

I felt safe because I was overweight and bulky. This was a great defense strategy for a young girl who didn't know how to help herself. I didn't have the resources or tools to share my experience and ask for help.

Even though I knew my condition was rapidly deteriorating, no one could help me. My parents were raised in a culture that didn't allow kids to act like I did, so my parents had no idea how they could support me. This made me feel even more alone.

These accumulated experiences led me to live in victimhood for many decades, wearing a 'I don’t care’ attitude and a mask of vulnerability. Self-pity was a way to manipulate others and get attention. I also used shame and blame to avoid responsibility. My drama, pain, self-hate, and drama became my addiction to get away from my true self. My days were filled mental spinning thoughts, judgments and resentments that led to overwhelm and disconnection. It's no wonder I smoked so much marijuana, binge-drank alcohol, and indulged emotionally eating. I couldn't be honest with myself. I was held captive in a fear-fat suit that I made.

Rock Bottom Radiance

At twenty-seven, I started smoking pot and drinking a lot. My sexual traumas gave rise to an addictive personality. I was numbing my body for years with drugs, alcohol, and drama. Any escape. It's not clear how I found online gambling but it became another form of escape. To be more specific, blackjack was my favorite game. I played it whenever I could, often until the wee hours of the morning. I was determined to win back my money when I lost it. I played more to make up the difference. I was ecstatic when I won money.

Could win more. It was a disaster.

In the end, I lost around 30000 dollars in just a few weeks. You read that right, $30,000. Yet again, I was at rock bottom. I was already depressed and my lifestyle was a mess. I had just lost more of my life.

Miraculously, I chose to stop. A moment of clarity occurred when I realized that I would never win my money back, because the house always wins. The reality of the situation was so bad that I couldn't see the bottom. I was scared to dig any deeper. Although I was not physically on the ground, I felt completely collapsed emotionally.

Defeated. Done. After fourteen years of addictions, depression, anxiety and PTSD, I was exhausted. And, now, this!

The moment I experienced a vision in my state of total collapse will remain with me forever. I saw myself in a dark tunnel. It seemed endless and was very long. I lay on the ground, wanting to give up. Then I lifted my head to look up at the tunnel's end. I looked up and saw that there was light in the distance. It was the end. Even though I could only see a glimmer of an end, it seemed so small that it almost looked like a star in a night sky.

In fact, it was my north star for the moment, and for many more over the next few decades. That moment was when I realized that the light symbolized hope and the possibility for happiness. I was suffering from depression so much that I wasn't sure if I would ever feel happy again.

That light reminded me of the possibility that it was waiting for me, as long as my efforts were directed towards it.

I began to crawl slowly, a bit like a baby. But it didn't matter. I was moving forward. A desire to see the light rekindled within me. I promised myself that I would crawl all the way, even if it meant I had to. It was then that I began to crawl faster and was eventually able stand. After that, I was able to take small steps and my speed increased. It was many years later that I finally made it out of the tunnel.

The light shone so brightly when I finally reached it. It was then that I realized the light was actually me. I was reaching for my own light, my own radiant self. I felt genuine happiness after two decades of depression. I was not happy all the times. Although I still struggled with sadness, anxiety and loneliness, I never imagined that I would be able to feel happy. I was overwhelmed by the accomplishments I had made and felt so proud. My burning desire to be happy had kept me going despite everything. This desire was what kept me going through all the times I wanted to quit (and there were many). I was especially devastated when my mom, my mother, suddenly died a few months prior to my thirtieth. Because I was not able to feel the emotions I felt, it was difficult for me to grieve her passing. Although I did use weed for some years to help me numb my pain, I kept my eyes on the prize with a fierce determination, despite all evidence to the contrary. If I took a few steps in the right direction, I knew happiness was possible. Even through the most difficult moments, I kept my faith and hope alive with my whole life.

Born To Be A Seeker

You can see that I am a seeker even in the most difficult, dark and uncertain moments of my life. My dad was my first spiritual teacher, and he continues to guide me. My mom was a strong leader and truthteller. And my stepfather was a grandmaster in Hung Gar Kung Fu and Qi Gong as well as a Chinese herbal medicine physician. Their presence has influenced my outlook on life and how I live it. I was able to follow their example and seek out the answers that I needed. They were brave in trying new things, introspective and service-oriented. I have also found myself acquiring these traits.

My Dad was a Jesuit priest in his youth. He eventually left.

He was displeased with the practice of the elders in the priesthood. He could not tolerate hypocrisy. He continued to explore spiritual texts, philosophies, and traditions over the years, eventually coming to the Tao and settling there. He has been an unwavering source of wisdom. We have spent many hours talking about yin, yang, energy laws and nature in the back rooms at the laundry room my parents still owned together. It was like my church. Students would visit the laundromat to benefit from his wisdom. His unconditional love inspires me to be more generous in my relationships. His energy and his teachings will always be the foundation of my work.

My mother was a biochemist, businesswoman and activist. She was always open to new ideas. She was sharp and curious about new opportunities. This was why my family was able to become middle-class. She was a strong woman, spoke her mind, cared not what others thought, and had the best laugh. She taught me the value of being a strong woman and leader. I continue to be inspired by her courage and fire.

I can still remember learning kung fu at my stepfather's martial art studio. It was located in the same building as our laundromat. They were located side-by-side and shared a door which connected them so that you could move from the back of the laundromat into the martial arts studio. They were close friends. This space was my home base, even in all the anger and outburst at my parents that I experienced as a teenager.

Even though Sifu was not able to communicate with me in words, as we didn't speak each other's language, his influence on my life was immense. He was my Chinese medicine doctor, and he inspired me to become a healer many decades later. He was teaching Qi Gong and students were seated in rows with their eyes closed. After he took a moment and cultivated his energy, he began pushing their bodies without touching them. It was the first time I saw the power of energy.

My mind was blown by the conversations I had with my dad about energy, and then seeing energy at work.

Martial Arts was another blessing as it changed the way I view things. In order to master the old school Kung Fu method of training, I had to observe every movement. It taught me to recognize the subtleties in people and situations, which has served me well.

As you can see, I was born as a seeker. As you will see, it has been quite a healing journey. This is my story. This is not a recommendation to you to follow my path; it's just to share more of myself with you.

My Healing Journey

My initiation to the healing world was through Acupuncture School. I learned so many things about myself, my body, energy, and about my culture. To help others was my way to helping myself. My experience as a clinician helped me to observe and research the mind-body connection and human nature. I was looking for answers and was eventually led to plant medicine.

Between the ages of 37 and 43, I went through an intense healing journey that led me to a new level of healing. This was initiated by two ayahuasca retreats that were held in 2013. Ayahuasca, a sacred plant medicine, is used in spiritual ceremonies by the Amazonian indigenous people. It provided me with an unspoken and unseen roadmap to my healing journey, guiding me with clear messages about what was next.

It directed me to Michfest (Michigan Womyn's Music Festival), where I found out that there were thousands of womyn who congregated on hundreds of acres of land, which was known as "the land". It was held every year in August, and that year was their 38th year. Imagine thousands of womyn camping together, enjoying workshops, food, laughter, partying and showering. It was a place where you could breathe and just be yourself. It was all built and created by womyn. It was a community effort that everyone had to volunteer to help keep the machine running. This created a richer sense of community. I felt my heart open during that time. It was the first time I felt such community and overflowing love with strangers. Eye contact, greeting one another with "hello sister" and "sister my sis", allowed me to feel naked in the woods while feeling secure in my own skin. Seeing other womyn embracing their unique curves, shapes and sizes inspired and motivated me to honor my true self more.

One day I was in the womyn tent of color and was sitting by the hammock with a group womyn. One of the men was reading through the program book and said that he could do a workshop called "Organic Meditation" in just fifteen minutes. "Would you like to go?" I felt my body light up, and it was an instant yes!

My body said yes immediately after I heard the women speak about how it allows you to let go and be open to receiving. This was exactly what my body desired, but I didn't know how.

When I returned to Brooklyn, I searched for OneTaste, a company that taught orgasmic mediation. I signed up immediately for their ten month coaching program, which was held monthly in San Francisco. I didn't care about travel, money, and commitment. It was what my gut said to me so I went for it.

When I arrived on the first weekend, I was totally triggered. I'd never seen so many white people in my entire life. Until this point, my closest friends were all black. However, I felt there was something more powerful for me to receive so I tried to be open-minded. Even though I was cautious at first, I was convinced by the practice by the end of the weekend. I loved Mastery so much, that I signed up to another program that would help you open your sex. I continued to explore their community and took all their programs over the next 2 years.

It was a very healing process and environment. I was able to connect with people in a more intimate and transparent manner than I had ever before. I was releasing so many of the sexual traumas and shames that had been stored in my body for more than two decades. I began to see myself differently, practicing using my voice and processing old emotions. I had previously been a control freak. I was disconnected from myself and other people. I was also a total control freak. I had sex only when I was high or drunk. I was able to let go of my fear and experiment in this sex-positive group, which allowed me to explore my sexuality in a way that helped me heal my trauma-filled brain.

This was the time I began to feel sexually and emotionally in touch with men again. Only eight years ago, I had been with women. It was a time when I could lean into large edges and listen to my body. This allowed me to discover sensations that were missing from a body that had been numb for many years.

Although I've been through many low points, it was an incredible experience to become a OneTaste NYC owner. Even though I disagreed with the management of the company, it forced my to look at myself and my insidious victim mentality. I was pushed to the edge by their extreme culture and had to look in the mirror. I was motivated to become sober emotionally, and quit smoking weed for a while. A sponsor helped me with the twelve-step program.

It was clear as day that I recall my first day in an AA facility. Just returned from MichFest's second festival, their forty-eighth and final. This time, however, was different from the previous. MichFest was my escape from drugs because I was so unhappy at OneTaste. I had never taken MDMA before this week. I was so upset that I used MichFest to escape. I woke up in tears five days later. I couldn't stop crying. I called OneTaste to get a massage. I tried other self-care methods but the tears would not stop. A OneTaste peer texted me and suggested that I attend an AA meeting. She didn't know what I had done at MichFest.

Although I have been to other AA meetings with the OneTaste community before, this was a new experience. The meeting was emotional for me. I was moved by the stories and the sharing. At the end of the meeting I was so emotional that I didn't realize that I was the only person in the middle of the room. I was surrounded by people standing in a circle with their hands. I joined the circle immediately and was overwhelmed by the kindness I received from complete strangers.

I ended up attending three meetings that day, and I decided to go sober. I felt much better that evening. That day, I felt the power in the rooms. So I found a sponsor who guided me through the 12 steps. Through her generosity and the steps, it was clear to me how selfish, manipulative, fearful, and resentful I was for most of my life. That was a gift.

I began attending Celebration Spiritual Center, a new type of church. They spoke my spiritual language, and they taught me what my father and I had always discussed. Modities such as the law of attraction and nature being our greatest teacher made it feel like home. This community gave me a sense lightness and comfort that was much needed. It was a difficult exploration of my shadowy side over the past few years, so it was good to find a balance with their inspiring services. I was touched by the songs, the teachings and the love.

Then, I was guided by intuition to enroll in a Women's Empowerment course taught and led by Regena Thomashauer (aka Mama Gena), a brilliant teacher of feminine power and author. Although I had heard about her through OneTaste, I never felt the need to enroll in her courses. I was secretly a judge of her and her community. I was nourished in a new way as I immersed myself into her teachings and the healing balm of sisterhood. This sacred container was where I learned to let go of my anger and grief and transform them into a powerful force called "turn on". These tools changed my life. Turn-on is an electrical current that occurs within you when you tap into the deepest, most expansive range of your feminine emotions and being. I learned new tools and modalities and began to transform my suffering paradigm into a pleasure paradigm. I also learned how to embody everything that I had within me.

The Catalyst

Since my first year at acupuncture school, there have been waves after waves of what I called awakenings. After a 2018 breakup, I felt like I had escaped the "matrix". As was the norm, it was a very dramatic breakup. This particular rupture was a catalyst for me to end my cycle of heartbreak and drama. I was ready to try something new.

I felt a huge weight of guilt after I broke up with him. It was as if he was abandoning me. I felt an intense urge to rescue him, fix and help him even though he had done me a great deal of hurt. It was my old friend martyrdom coming to visit me! My ego was in complete torture mode, trying to convince myself that I was a terrible person. I couldn't stop feeling guilty. I was mocking myself. Then, I had a moment of clarity and realized that you were making yourself responsible for his suffering. It has nothing to do wit you. He is responsible for his own actions.

When I heard my spirit, Pastor Yolanda introduced me to a miracle practice. She suggested that I try The Work by Byron Katie. It is a simple meditation process that allows you to see the truth within yourself. You can challenge one belief or thought at a time and your suffering will naturally dissipate as you ask each question.

Although I knew intellectually that my beliefs and thoughts were holding me back from my goals, something happened in my body when I did The Work. It was like I had changed from seeing my life in splotches to living in full technicolor. My vision became clearer and my mind was calmer. Through The Work, I experienced a series of 'aha' moments in my body. Two key insights changed my entire life. That was what I saw:

- I was addicted to suffering and drama because it was what I was used to and comfortable with, which meant that I was *choosing* to suffer.
- If it was true that this was a choice, then I had the power to choose something else!

Guilt was my perfect partner in healing me. Every time I felt it I knew it was a chance to experience the deeper emotions that were hidden beneath it. It was a blessing in disguise, because my ex tried to win me back by passive-aggressively trying to make me feel bad. There are no accidents. He was a mirror of what I needed to heal. Instead of feeling jaded or angry at him for acting like a child and allowing my feelings to fester, I took these opportunities to learn my boundaries. I continued to say no with firmness, love, and respect. I felt less guilty each time and my self-compassion grew. I felt stronger in myself.

I also included self-forgiveness. Instead of focusing on his forgiveness, I chose to forgive myself for the many ways that I contributed to the unhealthy dynamics between us. He was not exempted from responsibility for his actions. This means that I was responsible for the parts I played. This forced me to practice self-compassion I had never experienced before in my entire life. This was a drastic departure from how I used to operate.

After months of intensive deep diving belief work, my roots belief that I was responsible for all suffering and wellbeing of others began to dissolve. This allowed me to redirect my attention and energy away from others and let go of the need to lose weight. This was something I'd never been able do before.

Releasing the Weight

You may have assumed that this book was just another dieting book when you first picked it up. Surprise! It isn't. Instead, I want to show you how intuitively leading from a transformed belief system and connecting with how your body, mind and soul feel can help you effortlessly lose weight and bring you joy and fulfillment.

It is important to remember that I fell in love with myself long before I lost weight. I continued to love myself as I went along the journey. It wasn't about losing weight and loving yourself. This is not how it works. People often try it this way and either gain weight or feel uncomfortable in their new bodies.

Before I was able to share my martyr story, my physical life was inactive and full of unconscious eating habits. I hardly ever exercised. My life spans over forty years. I only had three brief periods where I exercised. In my teens, I attended a Kung Fu class taught by my stepfather for less than one year. I had been swimming for less than one year when I was 29 years old. Boot camp was something I did for around a year when I was 41 years old. I hated walking everywhere. I drove to NYC to work because I couldn't walk or take the train. Plus, I felt safer in my car. More hiding.

When I was a kid, emotional eating started. Food was my safety blanket. I was a foodie. I loved food and would clean up after myself.

One of my best friends joked that my father loved me because I would eat all his food, clean it, then go for second helpings. I ate without thinking. I ate whatever food came to my mind, and didn't think about it.

When I released my martyr story, my body began to tell me it was time for the physical work. It was now possible to listen to my body every step of the journey. I did things I didn't want to do, such as jogging. But my body said so, so I did it. Mirror work and intermittent fasting were two things that my body suggested to me. My body also told me to cut my bangs. It was so easy that I did it! I began to fall in love again with myself, and with the parts of me that I hadn't previously seen. The weight started to fall because my body and mine became best friends. It was a matter of trust.

I created a goal-setting system that kept me accountable to my goals. Because I understood how important it was to have a support group for my journey, I created one. In just five months, I had lost forty pounds and 15% body fat. I felt strong, confident, and alive!

The inside is the first place to heal. Anyone can release weight if they have enough willpower. Willpower is only temporary. What feels good and sustainable is what I care about. This is a living practice of self-love.

The Other Side

Because I did the work required of me, I am now on the other side from my traumas. It all ended in my gratitude. My traumas would have prevented me from being able to speak to you about releasing your body armor. I wouldn't have the ability to empathize and become a teacher, healer, and author. I wouldn't be able to experience my darkest moments as deeply as I have.

The depths of darkness I have loved into has a direct relationship to how bright my light shines. My ability to love my darkness and hold it in the light led to a greater sense of light inside me. Everyone has a history of suffering. But if it is kept hidden, it is impossible to love it. It is impossible to transform it. It must shine. It must shine. It must shine! This process of alchemy allows you to feel, taste and embody the light within you.

Now I am able to share the story of how it is possible to move around it and not through it. This opens up a world of possibilities that go beyond your wildest dreams. This is not just about the wealth you can create in your life through financial success, community, success, and the body of your dreams. Peace of mind, happiness, and connection are what I am referring to. This is the gift of taking your life journey into your own hands.

This book is written from the perspective of honoring my dark and my light, and all those who were part of my life, regardless of their appearance.

CHAPTER 3

Inside Out

"The whole cannot be well without the parts."

-- Plato T. The process I will show you is about uncovering who you really are beneath all the shame, pain, fear, and guilt that you've been holding onto. It's about remembering you are whole, and not needing to be fixed. While you may have to peel back the layers of protection you have built around you, you were created whole and complete.

According to what I have seen, many women like you are trying to find the dragon of healing. They hope that they can get out of this course with their lives changed. Even though you can attend the best seminars and have profound experiences with plant medicine, read all the self help books, and be mentored by great mentors, that doesn't mean you will achieve lasting freedom in life. There is no magic bullet. It is necessary to work in all areas - the mental, emotional, and physical. It's impossible to avoid it.

My observation is that women use their intelligence to attempt to solve their problems. This will not work, as intelligence is limited in its ability to get you far. Intelligence is the ability to understand and grasp a concept, as well as learn about important philosophies and practices. To create integrated and lasting shifts, it is important to cultivate, inhabit, and live fully in meditative states. This is not about meditation that you do in order to accomplish this work. I mean being connected to your inner world of emotions, thoughts and sensations every moment of your daily life.

My teaching method is based on yin, yang, and entry points. It is a way to take full advantage of the activations in your life, and use these activations for the digging work your spirit desires. Integrity and being present in these charged moments can make a difference. You will find the right path for you as you hold space for all of the possibilities. This is sometimes called "flow state" or working with the wisdom and the Tao.

Yin and Yang

As an acupuncturist, my goal is to treat the root cause. While the symptoms can be treated, the primary focus is on the cause of the imbalance. My dad is a Taoist spiritual therapist. Taoism is the basis of acupuncture.

Taoism is based upon nature and expressed through the relational dynamics between yin/yang and how these flow and interact. They are complementary, but they can be opposite.

Yin, the feminine, represents fluids (like blood), deeper inner aspects of self as well as the slower, more intuitive and receptive aspects of life and self.

Yang is masculine. It represents the qi, the outer aspects, the light hitting, and the structured and dominant aspects of life and self.

Taoism is grounded in nature and the flow of yin to yang. To understand how I transmit my teachings, you must first understand the nature and relationship of yin & yang.

If you examine the yin/yang image, the black is yin, while the white is the opposite. Each has a dot at the center with the opposite color.

This symbol represents the relationship between them. They are interconnected and can't be separated. They are interconnected and each other's movement is affected by the other. They are both energies that are connected and very alive. They change and fluctuate just like nature. This ancient wisdom can be incorporated and learned to help you connect to your flow. Yin and Yang are always in flow.

This dynamic is everywhere you look. Everything is a mixture of both. Each person, each project, each relationship. Within each person or thing lies another layer of yin/yang. It is possible to break down any thing into its yin and yang aspects. This information is vital to your progress through the process, as it will allow you to determine exactly where you stand in relation to the balance of both.

The beauty of the Tao is its inherent sense of compassion. There are no expectations about what should be or shouldn't be.

My teachings combine both internal and external (yin), as well as fluid and structured (yang), work. In keeping with this philosophy, the approaches have a balance between compassion (yin), and commitment (yang). It is all about balance, and how each element flows with the others. Each piece cannot be considered an isolated unit. They are all one and interconnect in a symbiotic manner. This is what creates peace and flow in your life.

Entry Points

It is amazing how humans are motivated to make major changes in their lives by desperation and not inspiration. Unexpected life events are bound to happen. It's all part of being human. We can learn from "negative" experiences, loss, and devastation, even though we do our best to avoid them.

As a child of immigrants, I was blessed with the gift of resourcefulness. I hate waste. I don't like to throw away food, money, and good old-fashioned pain. Many years ago, my dad taught me that challenges were gifts from the Universe. Do you want to throw it away or open that gift and discover what is waiting for you inside?

This was something that has remained with me throughout my life. I have made it a point to use the challenges of life to help me grow. It's like an emotionally leveraging system. These little and big life events can be used as stepping stones if we are willing to walk through it, rather than around it.

This was the beginning of my entry point process. The Universe is a co-creator with us and guides us in amazing ways when we allow our discomfort or pain to serve as an entry point to our healing. It's about being resourceful at the next level, tapping into the undiscovered world.

This advanced form of gratitude is something I practiced, and I found that I was able to reveal more of myself as a result. What I discovered was more love. Because heartbreak gives you the chance to feel and discover parts of yourself that have been hidden for years or even decades, it's why I believe that more love can be found in your life.

There are three types of entry points: mental, emotional and physical. Each realm has an entry point that can either be activated by thoughts, emotions, or sensations. An entry point allows you to explore deeper inside yourself and uncover the hidden parts. When something is suppressed, flow becomes blocked. You are operating from an unconscious place in your life. This is what I teach. It is meditative and alchemical. And transformative. Energetic flow occurs naturally when you work in all three realms.

Alchemy

Many people have told me stories about losing weight and then gaining it again because they didn't do the self-love work. It happens all the times. It is a common problem in our culture. This basically means you don't want to be there with yourself, no matter what, because it is too painful to feel the discomfort of your thoughts, emotions, and sensations. You choose to ignore, which eventually means you are numbing.

Alchemy goes beyond all of this. It is an alchemical process to walk through the portals that are opened when entry points become active. It is the act of bringing out the darkness and allowing you to be fully present. Love is found where there is presence. It takes courage to be present for the parts of yourself that have been neglected, pushed down and abandoned. This will be one of your most difficult decisions. But the rewards of investing in yourself in love and self-love will outweigh the risks.

Receiving All The Benefits

This book is divided in four sections. The Foundation, The Yin Portal and The Yang Portal are the four sections of this book. This section provides the foundation and preparation needed to enter the healing portal. The second section teaches you how to become a conscious practitioner, and activate your activated entry points. The third section focuses on self-care, goal setting, and turning on your body. The fourth section is about your journey out of the portal into a life of radiance, sustainable flow, and joy.

To make the most out of this book, you should open your mind and heart to reading. This book is an alchemical process that requires you to be open to seeing and doing things differently. This is a journey that will bring you miracles and I am here to help you navigate new territory. You will see places you have never seen before so be prepared to take the risk. My words will take you to the depths of your heart, mind, soul, and body. Do not try to figure out or understand anything with your intellect. Be present to the energy of my transmissions and you will receive the deeper messages I have for you.

After reading each chapter, take a few moments to be still and close your eyes for a while. Then you can let the messages of that chapter integrate into your body by being present with what is happening in your breathing.

After each ritual, I suggest that you take some time to acknowledge your source energy, your ancestors and your loved ones. A powerful way to end a ritual is to acknowledge your gratitude for the people who are loving you, supporting you, and leading you.

You are invited to read each chapter at your own pace. Notice when you resist, when you go too fast, or when you are not being kind to you.

A journal is a good idea to keep handy in case of an 'aha' moment or a question you need to ask. You can also write it down to remind yourself later.

As each chapter builds upon the previous, I recommend that you read them in order. Each chapter can be thought of as a stepping stone. After you have finished the book, you can practice blending the steps together to make a new way of living.

Notice that I say releasing weight rather than losing weight. Release weight feels more proactive and accountable, while losing weight seems more passive and less empowering. You are choosing to let go of something when you release it. You lose something and you want it back.

Last but not least, I want to stress that my method for losing weight is not about being thin. Because of our culture, we have been taught to believe that to be beautiful and fit the patriarchal and racist standards of beauty society has set for us. These messages won't serve your new magnificence or radiance. This is a journey I offer to help you reconnect with your inner self and live happily and peacefully in your body after years of living without it. Your goals could change dramatically as you go along this journey and try the rituals and exercises I recommend. You may think you want forty pounds. But once you have lost twenty pounds you will feel great and not desire to lose another pound. Perhaps you just fall in love with your body as it is. No matter what your goal, I want to help you create a happy, fulfilling life and a lasting, satisfying relationship with your body. I will show you powerful techniques that will allow you to tap into the unlimited potential of energy available to you, and all people on this planet. The ripple effects of love

My greatest desire is to see the world experience healing and love. Many people try to make positive changes in the world but give from a place that is empty, exhausted, fearful, overwhelmed, or resentful. None of these methods work. These may temporarily affect surface changes, but they are not sustainable over the course of a lifetime. My mission is to remind everyone that the only way to change the world is within each of us.

The micro and macro levels are the same. You see, what's happening inside is also happening outside. It would be natural for goodness to flow throughout the world if we all put our healing and connection to source energy, the universe, or any other term that suits us. Natural is the key word here. A genuine connection to love is the best way to bring about lasting and significant cultural changes. All of our interactions will change when we love ourselves. Our interactions with others, including our loved ones, friends, family, and communities, are more humane and profound. The kindness that we show to others naturally flows onto them, and it continues to spread from one person to another. This is a fundamental law that governs energy, and it is how we can make a difference in the world. Think about it! Think of the ripple effect of love that each person creates for others, and spreads outward.

Our culture is obsessed about external conditions. As a result, our brains have become conditioned and brainwashed by the lessons society and our ancestors have taught us. We have taken on lies after lies and accepted them as Truth with a capital "T".

These lies will make you think you're not worthy, desirable or lovable. These lies will convince you that you don't have to be perfect or do things perfectly, and you're not enough. While we will discuss how to change your stories and limit beliefs, first you need to be open to the possibility that you have been hypnotized. Without ever knowing it, we all have drank the proverbial Kool-Aid.

Understanding that your body is the most important part of loving yourself, I want you to know. Your body is the vessel that you were born into and the vessel in which you will eventually die. That is the only thing that can be changed. It's okay to love your flesh and be happy with it. You might think that if you don’t love your body, you are declaring war on yourself. It is essential to love all parts of ourselves, even the imperfect ones, in order to feel whole, alive, complete, and complete.

The Foundation

CHAPTER 4

Meet Your New Best Friend

Courage is the most important virtue of all because it prevents you from practicing any other virtue consistently.

— Maya Angelou

Into the Tunnel Ritual

The first step to navigating the portal is to ignite your internal engine. Imagine that you are driving in your car, and that you have stopped in front of a secret tunnel. The tunnel is a portal to healing and you're about to drive through. First, ensure your car has enough gas. Now imagine that you have checked your oil and balanced your tires. Imagine turning the ignition key on your car and lighting it up.

This sparks the engine and gets it moving. Your engine is now humming.

Take a look in your mirrors, and while you are at it, give yourself an eye roll.

Imagine a life where, just like driving an imaginary car, you take control of your actions and focus on what you can control: yourself. Are you ready? You need to buckle your seatbelt. It takes courage to take responsibility for your vehicle and your life!

Own Your Desires

To be willing to take on this new adventure, you must have a strong desire. You can't commit to anything if there is no passion or anchor connected to a larger vision. You can't. You can't.

If we are able to allow our bodies and spirits to express our desires, it is possible for us all to realize that everything is possible. You can be more specific about your desires. All of your senses are available. Allow yourself to get excited by the vision you can see in your mind's eyes. It is real! That knowing will cause a frequency vibration that will co-create the Universe with you - you'll receive all the support you need. The person you see in the vision is already within you. People are trying to make things from an intellectual perspective, but that won't take you far. Miracles can only happen if you bring all your senses.

"Desires act as a bridge between you and the greater power that is beyond you. Desires are the foundation of creation.

-- Regena Thomashauer aka "Mama Gena"

Desire Ritual

Take three deep, slow breaths while you sit in a private area. Allow your breath to move through your body. Relax and allow your body to breathe deeply.

You can now visualize how you want to feel in your body and in your life from this place of embodiment. Imagine how your life could look if you let go of your emotional and physical weight.

Where are you? What are you doing now? What are you wearing?

How does it feel?

This is your life. This is your life. This is your life. This is you. Get excited. Feel the joy.

After exploring for a while, you can take three deep breaths. Then slowly open your eyes. You can thank your higher power and the loved ones on the other side of you for supporting you during this experience.

Keep a journal of what you see and experience. Writing can help you to cement it in your body.

You can take it one step further by creating a vision board that reflects what you saw or felt. Have fun! Keep it in your favorite place until you are done.

Courage

Courage is a state of being totally and utterly loyal towards yourself. This requires you to be completely and utterly selfless in the most life-affirming manner possible. It means that you will give everything to yourself, without taking anything from anyone else. What makes you happy? What makes you happy? What makes you feel happy?

Courage is about embracing a warrior spirit and self-love. Prioritizing how you feel is the most important thing. This includes your children, your partner(s), work, and anything else. You will get stuck in a cycle that is all about taking care of others and feeling resentful. You will feel uninspired, unhappy, and drained if you don't put yourself first. You'll find yourself living for others, wondering about what happened and why your life feels so different from it five, ten, and even twenty years ago.

It takes courage to be yourself. It doesn't matter if your mind is full of obsessive thoughts, or if you are angry and full rage, it takes courage to be present in these places. Courage is also required to try new things. Bravery is the willingness to read and try out some of these rituals. One of my clients was afraid when I showed her the portal entry ritual. She thought she would be plunged into darkness and never emerge. It took courage for her to accept the challenge, despite all her fears.

Courage is required to be completely honest with oneself and to love one another unconditionally. It takes courage and commitment to have a deep, intimate relationship with your self and with the source of energy. This requires incredible courage to trust the process.

Each time I have experienced growth in my life in any way, be it in money, career, love, relationships or other areas, it was because I took a leap, jump or leap of faith. I followed my gut and took action. My life has been filled with many leaps of faith. Many people have doubted my sanity. But I knew that I had to trust my inner guidance system. To follow this deeper knowledge you must be a warrior. To hear this intuition, trust the process and believe that it will all come to you in due course.

Pleasure Researcher

Mama Gena introduced me to this term during her Mastery program. It struck me immediately because I love the idea of life being a huge'research project'. I have researched boundaries, how to give and receive, how to be a victim, and many healing modalities. While I have researched many different relationships, careers and places to live, I never considered researching pleasure. It was a big decision for me to pursue a career as a pleasure researcher. This is because patriarchy has made women choose to suffer and believe it is their only way of life. A woman who prioritizes pleasure will find that she is able to explore what actually lights her up and not just what numbs her. This will lead to a more fulfilling life. Being a pleasure researcher requires courage and bravery.

My weight-loss journey began as a pleasure research project. Why? Why? Because I had tried to lose weight in the past and it was miserable and frustrating. This time, I wanted to find joy in my body. Everything changed when I added "turn-on", and "pleasure" to the mix. Are you able to identify what brings you joy? If not, I suggest you do some research.

Real pleasure doesn't just mean doing what you want, when you want. You don't have to eat all the Halloween candy your children give you.

I don't know if you're curious, but I love being curious and I enjoy trying new things. The whole game changes when you make weight release a research project. It's an experiment.

Let's get started! Grab your lab coat or pleasure researcher hat and let's dive into the details.

Pleasure Research Ritual

Get out some paper and a pen to write down everything that brings you joy, from the small things to the big things.

Next, write down everything on your to-do list that makes you feel anxious or want to put off.

Do one thing that you enjoy before you start working on a task. This will increase your joy and stimulate your body's electricity.

I hated doing taxes, until I started to enjoy them with dance breaks. Every twenty minutes, or whenever I felt like I was losing energy or feeling irritable or foggy, I would take a break.

Making Yourself # 1

You must first choose yourself to be able to perform this alchemical self-loving work. There is no other way. It is essential that you make a commitment for your enjoyment and peace. You will have to make difficult decisions about downsizing.

simplifying your life. This means you will need to say no to friends, family, or experiences you don't want to accept. This means you will view your time, energy, and space as commodities that aren't up for negotiation. It's not possible!

This commitment is key to making the changes you need to lose weight.

You can choose yourself by slowing down and asking yourself what priorities you have. Keep only the important things. Let go of the things that aren't working in your life and don't add unnecessary stress. Get rid of clutter in your life, mind, and space. You can let go of all distractions and make room for something new. You can make wise choices by focusing on the important things that are most important to you. Then, observe the impact of having this space on your life.

Marie Kondo That Sh*t Ritual

Get a bird's-eye view of your entire life. Which parts of your life are more spacious than others? These are some areas that people often clutter up their lives:

- Does your home feel cluttered?
- Are there a gazillion things you need to do?
- Are there events on your schedule that you aren't excited about?
- Do you bring work home with you or you stay at work late all the time?

Choose the area that you feel is most important or exciting to clear out. Start to declutter what doesn't "spark joy", as Marie Kondo would call it, and those that aren't prioritized.

Feel the openness and gratitude that has been given to you.

Take a moment to be grateful for your brave act of letting it go.

You are also committing to yourself when you say 'yes to the process. How can you say yes to the process when you have failed at it before? You decide to change your mind and fall in love with it. It becomes an adventure and a passion. You are so focused on what you want in your life, that you love every moment of it.

This book will help you learn how to surrender to the process I have laid out. It's unlike any weight-loss process you've tried before. This isn't a one-time deal. This is a lifetime's work. It's not about losing weight; it's about building an intimate relationship with your body.

Making the Choice

Do you choose you first? This is the most important question of the book, and it was the one I had to answer when I found myself at crossroads. I looked ahead and saw the fork in my path. I chose the left path, which was the one that I have been on for my whole life. It was full of bad energy and all my failures. Then, I turned to the right and saw a new path I hadn't taken before. It was a completely new area with many questions, but there were also many possibilities. To make my life change in the way I desired, I had to make the radical decision to prioritize me no matter what. I chose the right path. Which path will you choose?

Crossroads Ritual

You can sit in a private, quiet space. Take a few deep, relaxing breaths and close your eyes.

Imagine yourself at a fork in the road.

Imagine the two paths. Is there any trees? Is it empty? What is in the distance? It's worth taking a few moments to truly take it all in.

Take each one one at a while. The left path is the first. You have already taken this path. You can take as much time as necessary to observe and feel the changes that occur when you focus your attention. What images, words or sensations come to mind? When you feel complete, focus your attention on the right direction and do the same. Be patient and enjoy the journey.

After you have taken in all the energy, switch your attention to the other paths and compare their energies and scenery. What are their differences? What do they think of each other?

Keep your eyes closed and ask yourself "which path should I take?" Only if you have a "left" or a "right" answer can you allow your inner voice the opportunity to speak. This is usually the first answer that comes to your mind and feels good in your body. While your mind might try to convince and enter, it should stay where your body is.

After you have received your answer, take some deep breaths and then open your eyes.

Finally, thank you to your higher power and your loved ones for allowing space for this exploration.

Congratulations if you have chosen the right path! Keep going to the next chapter.

Congratulations if you chose to follow the left path. This will keep you here until your self-respect is restored. It is a good thing to recognize that you resist prioritizing your own needs. Clarity is the best thing. You may have thought that you were ready for this meditation but now you see you are not. This is a good thing because it allows you to be completely honest with yourself. Before, you tried to convince yourself or force yourself into something that was not right for you at that moment.

Instead of dwelling on your shortcomings or being self-critical, I encourage you to engage in another ritual to support you in this commitment.

Left Path Ritual

Write for ten minutes why you chose the left path. Open and honest about what is holding you back. Take the time to feel what is causing you pain. Allow yourself to look at the beliefs and reasons that prevent you from choosing you first. Be aware of excuses you make for not prioritizing yourself. All of your resistances should be written down. List everything that you can think of that might be holding you back.

Once you feel satisfied, go back to the beginning of the chapter and do the Desire Ritual. Connect with your desire to remove your body armor. Feel the desire to shed your body armor. When you are ready, perform the Crossroads Ritual once more.

They can be done back-to-back or next day. While you don't want your system to be overloaded, you don't want it to go unnoticed. You will gain more clarity and maybe even the desire to try something else.

When you have completed a ritual, please take a moment and thank your higher power, your loved ones, and yourself for allowing this moment in your life to unfold.

You might be asking yourself, "Why are you so hard on me?" You love me, so I don't mind being tough. My job is set you up for success.

To do that, you need to be grounded and make your joy and happiness your top priority. If you don't commit, all the steps will seem difficult and will prove to be very difficult. It's not about making you do something you don't like. It's about you feeling the desire to do the work.

The Yin Portal

CHAPTER 5

Learning To Be With Yourself

"The wound is where the Light enters."

— Rumi

Entry Points Imagine you're a detective and you are hot on the trail of solving a mystery that you were hired for. You have been finding clues and are on the hunt to see where they lead. That is what an entry point is. A clue that leads you into a spot that wants attention. They give you an opportunity to be present with what is wanting to arise from within you.

These three realms are where entry points are activated: emotional (emotions), mentally (thoughts), physical (sensations). They can trigger a range of responses, from numbing and losing control to a wide variety of emotions. However, you can use these entry points to your advantage and to help you uncover more about yourself. Get ready to investigate!

Although they may be gold nuggets, they are often overlooked as the problem. We can take back our power if we see them as the perfect portals to alchemizing. This is about being resourceful, and using these gifts to transform the once negatively charged energy into power. Your energy will rise if you can transform these powerful entry point activations. You can harness the energy contained in "negative" activations to transform them into something more useful.

It is one thing to be capable of connecting with the physical, emotional, and mental realms separately; it is quite another to be able connect with them all simultaneously. People tend to avoid one or more realms and focus their energies on the one they feel most comfortable in. It is possible to avoid the work that has the greatest impact if you focus on your comfort zone.

You may believe that you feel an emotion when it arises but in reality you are focusing on a negative storyline and thereby preventing the emotion from being felt.

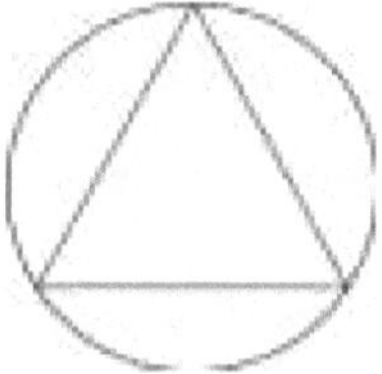

The circle connects only if you do the internal work at each entry point. The circle represents flow. This is the balance between yin/yang, and being able to trust your inner guiding system. Living from a place where you surrender to your intuition is key. You will receive the abundance that comes with that openness. In the midst all that is going on in your world, you feel the divine within.

Imagine that each activated entry point opens up a spiraling portal. Either you choose to go through it, or you can choose to continue to avoid it. Now is the time for you to find your courage and honor your deepest truths, even if they haven't been explored yet.

This is the process that I use to guide you through these portals. The following chapters break down the process for each realm in detail.

It is important to remember that activations can be powerful and worth your attention. You could experience small moments like someone looking at you in a particular way or more profound experiences such as death. All of them deserve respect. In my experience, the smaller activations are just as powerful since they happen all the time. You think you can sweep all those opportunities under the carpet? This is the non-wasting first generation Chinese woman!

My practices are designed to help you cultivate your capacity to be alone and to keep yourself safe. The practice can be used to improve any aspect of your life.

Before you dive into the portal, the first thing to do is to get you started with meditation.

Sitting Meditation

Meditation is one of the best methods to travel through the portal, and to cultivate a connection with the yin/yang flow.

Meditation is powerful because it allows you to receive so many benefits in one practice. Meditation helps you cultivate compassion, increase your awareness and expand your awareness.

Although I was a practitioner all my life, it took me years to understand what an actual practitioner was. All practitioners are practicing something at all times, conscious or unconscious. Being a conscious practitioner means that you can see and act on what is happening in your thoughts and behavior in real time.

My entire life I have been a victim to my own self-pity, blaming others and being a control freak. After taking self-development classes and learning more about the power and importance of our intention, attention and intention, I realized that it was all down to being a conscious practitioner.

Meditation can also help to restore the body. Relaxation is essential for your body to be able to heal and allow the cells to function normally. It also allows the emotional body to let go of what it holds onto. Meditation can be used to help with insomnia, anxiety, depression, and other physical ailments that are caused by stress. Numerous research studies have also confirmed that stress is a major factor in creating diseases in the body.

Meditation can help you be more aware of what's going on inside. You can see and feel things you didn't know you could. Your awareness and mindfulness will naturally expand. My entire life changed after I started to meditate. It was not surprising that I hit a low point and decided to start my meditation practice. I felt more grounded, and I was more patient and kind with myself. Clarity replaced my confusion and fogginess. In my daily life, I was able to connect with the idea that progress is possible, and not perfection. My meditation practice has evolved and impacted me in profound ways over the years. Now I feel the divine power and love that is available to everyone, living inside me.

I recommend Stress Less, Accomplish More, Emily Fletcher, regardless of whether you are a beginner or a seasoned practitioner. This book is great for both beginners and experienced meditators. It teaches you a simple meditation technique and encourages you to stick with it. The most important thing for first-time meditators is to realize that meditation is not a bad practice. It is not possible to get rid of all your thoughts. Meditation is not about being a thought-free state. Meditation is not about being a mindless activity. It's about cultivating more presence with oneself. You will feel more connected to yourself, and better equipped to handle stress.

Sitting meditation is meant to increase your ability to hold space for you so that your daily life can be transformed into a meditation practice.

Meditation Ritual

Choose a quiet and comfortable place to sit. For twenty minutes, set a timer (I suggest the "Insight Timer") and close your eyes. Take three deep, slow breaths. Feel your body and be aware of your senses. Take three deep breaths and notice any sensations you feel in your body. Next, focus your attention on your breath, or on a simple mantra like Om, peace, and relax. You can bring your attention back to your mantra or breath every time you think of something. This is not a way for you to stop thinking, but to practice being compassionate and non-judgmental.

This is a circular motion that includes the inhale/exhale, and the process of noting your thoughts and gently but firmly bringing yourself back into yourself. It's yin yang flow.

Take a moment to thank Source energy and your loved ones who support you on the other side of the bell when it rings.

Being a Conscious Practitioner

Being a conscious practitioner means living in a state of meditation and creating space for yourself. This does not mean that you are a monk, nun or saint. This means you are aware and highly tuned and can make conscious decisions throughout your day. This means you are meeting yourself right where you are.

You will find a peaceful place to go into a meditative, explorative state. It's an adventure. It's a journey into uncharted territory that allows you to learn more about yourself and experience more of the life you have been living. It is not a linear process. It is fluid and intuitive, and meditative. It's not possible to do it wrong, it's a process. This way you will see the potential for positive change in your life. You can focus on those moments that aren't being used or transformed into something great. It's not always easy, but it is possible. It takes practice. It's a practice! Before you start, you are already off the hook. It is amazing! It's so easy to just play!

This conscious practitioner practice has been broken down into six easy but powerful steps that can be used to activate an emotional, mental or physical entry point. The general process is described below. In the following three chapters, I will share specific rituals that can be used in each realm.

This practice focuses on cultivating compassion and love for others and yourself. Love is the energy binding force.

1. Creating Space

De-clutter your life and learn to be present with yourself. You can feel what is happening right now, without focusing on the past. If you're consuming your time with work, shopping, social media, TV, social media, TV, or other mental obsessions, you will be unable to feel the moment. Avoidance is a form of avoidance. You are making it more difficult to process and integrate the events in your life by not allowing yourself quiet moments and stillness. All of your life experiences accumulate in your system, making you feel stuffed and cranky. Many people are so busy and distracted that it's difficult to slow down and make space for themselves. This is similar to a life-long habit of eating too much and feeling satisfied. How can you possibly know what the other side is if you have never experienced it?

One of my clients had already taken several self-development courses but she wasn't sure what it meant to make space for herself. We did a session together and I guided her through various visualization meditations and breathing exercises. She had avoided meditation because she was afraid of the unknown. Fear of falling into despair, not being able get out of it, then having to put on a cheerful face for the rest of the world in order to be productive. Ironically, her constant feelings of despair was caused by her inability to be present with herself. It was then that she realized that creating space and self-care activities were not the same thing. Self-care activities are still "doing", but not necessarily "being". This was yet another task to cross off her list. She was great at it.

She felt out of control as she tried to help her be more present with herself. Anxiety, sweaty palms and racing heart all increased.

Meditation was something she avoided like the plague. She was afraid of her inner child returning to this world. It was safer to keep her tender side, as well as her emotions, hidden. Her adult identity was so wrapped up in her ability of control, success and productivity provided the perfect validation for her to keep going along these lines. These were perfect excuses to not create space.

Here are some ideas to help you create space and time for yourself:

- Stop checking your phone and social media randomly. Use the "screen time" app on your phone to schedule allotted time for social media, etc. The average amount people check their phone is 80 times a day. Average amount of time on social media is 30 minutes a day which equals 22 days out of the year!
- Stop consuming information and start practicing what you already know.
- Slow down. Literally. With your movement, with your speech, with everything.
- Declutter your schedule and your to-do list of things that are not priorities.
- Take moments of deep breaths throughout the day at work.
- Go for a walk with your phone off.

- Walk slower and take in the environment around you.
- Dance breaks.
- You can hire a nanny to look after your children for a few hours each week.
-

To prepare yourself for the day, create a morning ritual that includes meditation and journaling.

- Create an evening ritual and shut down screens early to prepare your mind and body for sleep.
- Do one thing at a time (no multi-tasking).
- You can say no to everything you don't want to do.
-

You can replace TV or social media with your time.

Essentialism: A Disciplined Pursuit Of Less is a great resource for how to simplify your life and lead a more fulfilling existence. Greg McKeown has it.

Being with the Breath

Breathing is the most powerful and simple way to create space. Inhaling expands your chest, creating space. Exhaling ground you. Conscious breathing is a way to bring presence and focus into the present moment. There are many types of breathing. Long, slow breaths. Fast quick breaths. After inhaling, hold the breath. Keep track of your exhale and inhale counts. For simplicity, count your inhale and exhale for seven seconds. This is when you are focusing on creating space with the breath.

The natural consequence of creating space and time is that you will be more aware of your energy tanks. It is the most valuable commodity we have, and it is important to treat it accordingly. You must pay attention to how much energy you have to do the deep work. People spend their energy in an endless cycle when they are on low levels of energy. You will be able to work hard and live the best life possible if you keep your tank full.

You have the power to decide what you want to do with your time and how much you put into your tank. This book will help you organically. Resentment used to be my main focus. I was a resentful person. It would make me resentful and obsess over it. It was no wonder that I was always tired.

2. Noticing

Many years ago, my dad taught me the art of notice. It is imagining your physical self at the moment, and then your higher self is on top of a mountain, looking down at your physical self. The higher self is able to see everything clearly and lovingly. She simply watches, trusts and knows what is. She watches your thoughts, emotions and behavior.

It is a way to practice mindfulness, which means paying attention to the things that are changing. Your life is always changing, and you are constantly moving. You will notice the changes and increase your awareness. You will notice more of what you think and feel more emotions. You can notice your inner thoughts and connect to the moment by noticing. This will allow you to determine if an entrypoint has been activated. Once you are able to do this, you can choose how you respond. Instead of reacting to situations, you bring conscious choice to each moment. Your ability to see the subtleties in yourself will improve with practice.

Noticing Ritual

While you go about your day, pay attention to how you feel. Ask yourself questions and take a moment to notice what your body is telling you. Throughout the day, continue to perform this check-in. You don't have to change or address any situation. Simply observe.

Thank you for taking the time to check in after each visit.

3. Attention

Did you ever notice that the things you pay attention to seem to have a magical effect of making your life more meaningful? Because we have total control over our attention, it is our greatest asset. You can choose which focus you want to pay attention to. It's entirely up to us. Nobody can get into your head and tell you what to do. This can be either good or bad, depending on how you view it.

It is good to realize you have control over your own life. It is bad when you prefer to be in victim consciousness. If you start obsessing over whether this person likes or hates you, you can shift your focus to all the wonderful friendships in your life. This is better than trying to track down their social media accounts to see if they hate you.

You will never be able control the thoughts, feelings, and actions of others. However, you have some control over the things you think, feel and do. That's a gift. This clarity will allow you to make a change in your life.

We are a distracted race. This is a result of our culture of multitasking, rushing and technological over-stimulation. Do you notice that your thoughts are constantly moving and that you don't have any control over them? It is because you have been practicing distraction all your life. You can change your habit of being distracted by the same thing. It's similar to building a muscle. It is not possible to expect that just going to the gym once in a while will build the muscles you desire. It will take practice and consistency. It's not just for sitting meditation, but throughout your life. This might seem daunting. However, the alternative to being dependent on your mind is not only uncontrollable, it can also be very frustrating. Imagine the possibilities when you can control what you focus your attention on. There are many possibilities.

Sitting meditation and focusing your attention on one subject is a great way to cultivate your attention. You can bring your attention back onto the subject if you are distracted. You are extending the time that your attention is on something or someone. This means that you can only do one thing at once, which is what we call creating space. You can do it with your thoughts, with a conversation, on a project, at work or in any other situation. You can also see inside yourself and decide what you want to focus your attention on.

Here are some examples of how you can attract your attention:

- Looking at anything for an extended period of time, such as, watching the faucet drip.
- Repeat the same mantra over and over.
- Pay attention to how your breath feels as it moves in and out your nose.

- If you're obsessing, put your attention on another thought.

You must keep practicing no matter what. To release your emotional and physical weight, you have to accept that you are the only one who can control it. It is in your best interests to improve your concentration and focus. Otherwise, it will be chaotic.

4. Curiosity

This practice and life will be easier if you have a childlike, beginner-like mind. The vibration of adventure is completely changed when you are able to explore and inquire. Imagine you are in a foreign country that you have never been to before. Imagine if you approach a new country with curiosity and fascination, rather than with a closed mind and indifference. You are more open to the unknown and less focused on a certain outcome. You see the world in a completely new way. You realize that the beliefs you have been so insistent about believing are false. It turns out that your entire existence is built on false beliefs. You discover answers you didn't know you needed. You discover emotions hidden in the cracks, and you are able to hold them. Because you want to find the hidden treasures beneath the surface, you actively engage with your body and not ignore it. You are open to new possibilities. Your willingness to learn increases. The Universe will surprise you when you're in a state that is open to inquiry. Because there is more space to explore, your intuitive "spidey senses" grow. If you are curious it means you are open to seeing, hearing, or feeling something new than what you have ever experienced, heard, or felt.

It's almost like you live in a box, and you have tunnel vision. This is telling the Universe you don't want to expand because you live in a box.

It is difficult for intelligent women to let go of what they believe they know. This is because their intelligence has created success and the life they live. It was quite shocking to realize that my spiritual and emotional intelligence was keeping me from achieving my goals. This is why curiosity is the antidote. It shows you are open to learning. When you are truly open, teachers, answers and help will always come. Sometimes you will happen to stumble across a book you've been meaning to read for years, and it turns out to be exactly what you need. You might hear someone speak truthfully and answer a question you have been contemplating for days.

Inner Child Ritual

Do you recall when you were young? This is the energy I'm referring to. Your inner child is eager to explore. Let her. Reflect on a time when you were young, playful and curious about something new. Imagine you are in that place. Is that at home, in the park, or in school? How did your hair look? What did you wear? Who was there? Put yourself in the shoes of that little child and look into her eyes. Feel the excitement, anticipation, and exploration she may be feeling. Get in touch with her now. Connect with her curiosity. Notice her willingness to take on new challenges. Notice her willingness to have fun and openness.

When you feel complete, you can thank your inner child. They have shown you what is possible when we are open to curiosity. Your higher power and loved ones on the other side should be thanked for allowing you to connect with your inner child.

5. Pivoting

Another thing my dad taught me many years ago that I love is the one-degree shift. He said that a one-degree change can lead to a totally different path. One-degree can have such an impact. Like all meditations, power is in the subtleties. It's not about forcing yourself to do something or making huge moves. You can tune into your moment and choose to make a conscious decision to go to the best spot to reconnect with yourself.

You can adjust if you see yourself drifting from the flow. Adjustments can be a powerful act to increase awareness and make choices. It's often the sum of small changes that you make over time that makes the greatest impact. Most people find it difficult to make big adjustments unless they've done the hard work required to make them happen. It is possible to take a few small steps at a time. You will gain muscle as you practice and you will eventually be able make larger and more drastic adjustments. It is important to be open to yourself wherever you may be.

Imagine that you are driving down a two-lane road and want to make a U-turn. To turn the car around, you'll need to slow down and make small adjustments. This is also true for your mental state and overall well-being.

You can ask yourself: What can I do right now to feel more at ease? Your adjustment might have been to tell your self to calm down in the past. This is an example of how too large a pivot can cause you to be out of alignment and make it harder for you to understand what you need at that time. Five deep, slow breaths would make the perfect pivot. Maybe crying your eyes out would make the perfect pivot. The perfect pivot might be to make a big leap of faith. This pivot step requires you to tune in to where you are at the moment and what you need. Is there a sweet spot? The sweet spot could be to take a sharp turn. It all depends on your location. The only way to find out is to practice meditation and learn about yourself.

One of my clients was always trying to do it "right" and trying to figure things out. She was trying to hard. I said to her, "You're trying too hard!" Then I explained the pivoting tool. She was able to see that she was trying to make huge turns, when she really needed to just shift one or two degrees. She was able to focus on her breath and make small shifts. It was amazing to her how this small pivot reduced her anxiety and improved her well-being.

Pivoting Ritual

When choosing a pivot, it is important to honor where you are at any given moment. It is the perfect thing to bring you closer to your body, and your presence. It could be anything. Here are some powerful pivots to help you get through those moments when you really need it:

- Breath.
- Dance break.
- Take a walk, feel your feet and enjoy the beauty of the outdoors.

- Choose another thought that is closer to alignment that is believable to you in that moment.
- Put your hands on your heart and tell yourself, "It's ok to feel this emotion right now."

You will be closer to alignment if you make a conscious choice to pivot in a resonant manner. You will be able to make another conscious decision to pivot. As you practice, you will be able to make more pivots.

6. Digestion

My experience has taught me that people need to take time to process and digest what they have learnt. Imagine yourself at a buffet and eating endless amounts of delicious food. Even though you are full, you continue to eat. What happens next? What happens? You feel sick. Don't wait to feel full. You should take the time to chew and digest each bite so that you can fully enjoy every moment. Being aware of your ability will not only help you in real-life eating but also your internal processes. You will be able emotionally and physically to notice how full you feel if you practice the habit of noticing.

When you look at the digestive system in its entirety, it requires time to rest and digest. Your body can recover and absorb all nutrients by fasting between meals. Your body needs energy to digest the food and transport the nutrients to the right places. You will overload your body if you eat every two hours. Your body will wonder if it is okay to relax, as it is working overtime. Your emotional body is going through the exact same thing. In a single day, so much can happen. Consider this. Every day, you need to take in all the happenings, emotions, and events. You will experience many transitions, especially if you are a woman committed to personal growth. People get stuck in transitions because they are entering into new experiences. This can cause anxiety and decrease trust. Because you can feel uncomfortable symptoms if you are physically stuffed, this is where digestion comes in. You can become energetically constipated if you don't eat well. There are many ways digestion can occur. My favorites are gratitude, celebration, seeing the good in the "bad". These tools will keep your energy high. These tools are like probiotics for your energy!

Gratitude Ritual

Begin a gratitude practice by writing down what you are grateful for every day in your journal. Every morning, write three. Don't stop there. You will find many things to be thankful for as you travel the globe. When you see something that sparks your gratitude, take a moment and say "thanks" It is important to allow your gratitude to expand to your whole being. This is the secret ingredient. It is not enough to write, speak or think about it. It must be felt.

Examples of gratitude:

- I am grateful for the stranger that held the door for me.
- It was a great find.
-
- It is a blessing to feel good about my body.

It was a blessing that I decided to take a shower today, instead of rushing to finish my to-do list.

- I am grateful that I said “I love you” to my partner today even when I was upset.
- I am grateful for the sun shining on my face.
- Thank you for your warm and safe home.

Celebrating is the second way I love digesting information. Celebrate everything. I don't mean the little wins, but the big ones. There is nothing too small to be celebrated, even the small ones. Milestones do not have to be big events like running a marathon. You can simply celebrate that you accomplished something new. If that means you were able meditate for the first-time, that you didn't emotionally eat as much, that you took the time to connect with yourself instead of reacting, then those are all reasons to celebrate.

When I started a celebration routine, every "negative" thought I noticed was celebrated. This is radical because it's a way to celebrate the fact that we have been conditioned to blame ourselves and others when we do something "bad" or are not nice to them. Because I was so excited to see things I hadn't seen before, I celebrated. That's huge. It was a process. Every step, every moment and every choice that I made makes a difference.

When I was running my first 5k race, I remember the moment. I was freezing cold in the water and didn't make my goal of 10 minutes per mile. These thoughts told me I wasn't training hard enough and that I had failed. Then I realized that this moment was my own and decided to celebrate the fact that I completed the race in inclement conditions and for being able to notice my judgment while it was taking place. I was able to recognize my judgments and have the space to learn more about myself. These small moments are more powerful than what you think because they add up to create momentum.

Celebration Ritual

You can celebrate by writing down all your accomplishments, sharing them with your community, having a fun celebratory dance break or looking in the mirror. Feel it. Get giddy! You just accomplished something you never thought possible. That's huge. Bravo! Applaud yourself. Give a cheer with your name on it.

Examples of celebrating wins:

- I celebrate that I started dating again!
- It's a great feeling to have a new belief about limitations!
-
- It is a great feeling to know that my intuition was right!
-

I love to create a boundary at work!

It's a great thing that I didn't feel the need to eat donuts at work when I was feeling stressed!

- I celebrate that I meditate daily now!
- When someone compliments me, I say thank you!

- I celebrate sharing more of myself with my friends!

When I was done writing a chapter, or when I had completed a difficult section, I would celebrate. My favorite thing to do was jump on my trampoline and shout out to my mirror "You did it!" Yayy! You are so proud! Sometimes I would dance to the song of my choosing. Sometimes I would just feel the joy and let myself be engulfed in the satisfaction of my achievement.

You can become a miner for the good, even when it's not good. This is possible by learning to look for positive things in places you wouldn't normally see. A few months back, my boyfriend split with me. I allowed myself to feel my emotions and to grieve the breakup. I did mental work to question the limiting thoughts in my mind and took extra care of myself. I chose to see things from a bird's eye view. His letting go was what propelled me into my next level of purpose work, and it is why this book was written. I was both grieving him and mining the experience for gold. You can do this with both big heartbreaks and small slights and annoyances. When you're tapped into, you can digest everything in your life and take in any nourishment that is available.

Conscious practice is about being present in the moment, and not about achieving a desired outcome. It's not about making things happen the way we want them to. It's about feeling, listening and then acting on your intuitive instincts. They are all there - we just have to be aware of them. People often have trouble listening because their ego is so loud it can become like a radio station in their heads. It's there all your life, and you don't even realize it. This will allow you to take control of the radio dial.

CHAPTER 6

Go Through, Not Around (The Emotional Realm)

"I believe that one reason people hold on to their hatreds so stubbornly, is because they know that once hate is gone they will have to deal with the pain."

James Baldwin Many women think they are in touch, but have a difficult time having an honest, open, and vulnerable relationship with their own emotions. Although this may sound difficult to believe, our minds can be very complex and will do whatever it takes to prevent us from being with ourselves.

Alchemy is about holding yourself accountable to your highest levels of compassion and approval. You cannot expect freedom from putting pressure on yourself, worrying about your actions, worrying about them, or controlling them. This is the old version of you. By shedding the layers of repressed emotions that have accumulated over years, you are able to discover your true self. This is the you that's been there all along and waiting for you to take it. Radical trust is a new way to trust yourself.

Connecting to our emotions allows us to connect with our intuition more deeply. Emotions can be good. They are entry points. When activated, they will tell us where we are and what we need. It's a lot like a compass. You will be able to trust your emotions once you have a better relationship with them. Because I was emotionally, I believed I was doing the emotional job. You don't have to be emotional to do the emotional work. These are two distinct things. So what I discovered was that I was an emotionally vulnerable child and was often in a victimhood mindset. Instead of being a mature, grounded adult, I let the little girl in my, who was angry and hurt, lead.

Signs you are emotionally unmature:

- You don't hold yourself accountable for your actions and blame others.
- You're fearful about everything and expect things to shift without doing the work.
- You try to control and manipulate the people or experiences around you so you can get your preferred outcome.
- You are unable to see your projections onto others.
- Because you expect others to be more like you, you become resentful.

- You use your woe is me stories to get attention from others by way of colluding and commiserating.
- You self-sabotage almost anything that has the potential for joy and fulfillment.
- Signs that you're emotionally mature:
- Take responsibility for your actions, and take a deep look within.

- You trust the process and are willing to do the work.
- You allow people to be who they are and are able to accept them along with all of the experiences in your life.
- You see how you project onto others and use that clarity to see deeper parts of yourself.
- You are a sovereign being because you know that you have no control over other people. You are able to keep the focus on you.
- You are attracted to people who will tell you the truth when you are off balance.
- You are aware when the ego wants to self-sabotage and you use the necessary tools to make sure you don't allow it to.
- You're learning how to become an adult that holds space for your inner child so that you can more masterfully hold space for yourself in the grittiest of moments when the immature parts of you want to act out or hide.

Pain versus Suffering

There is no such thing as suffering. Feelings can include pain. It is normal to feel pain. Being a human being means that you will experience pain. It is part of our life. We cannot control the events in our lives and will feel pain. Suffering is a completely different animal.

Suffering occurs when we believe the stories and thoughts that our ego creates to keep us spinning. Suffering prevents us from experiencing the deeper emotions. The good news is that even though pain is real, you have the option to choose to not suffer. This is what you can do instead:

- Identify whether you are in pain or in suffering.
- Feel your emotions (emotional realm) if you're in pain.
-

Ask yourself if you are suffering.

My devastating breakup was followed by the deaths of two of my furry friends, Ceba my cat and Baby my dog. Every time I saw how my ego created a story about me telling myself that I should have done something differently in their final days, weeks or months. It was almost unbearable. That is suffering. I began to notice that I was suffering from self-inflicted pain and started questioning the beliefs that my ego tried to convince me to believe. It became apparent that I was creating a feeling of guilt by avoiding the raw emotions beneath, the grief. This is called pain. To protect you from feeling emotions (pain), the ego creates lies (suffering). Visually, I can see the energy of raw emotions hidden in the darkest and smallest places in my gut. The lies act as a damp blanket to prevent you from getting into those spaces.

Once I saw the truth, it was clear to me that I needed another moment of clarity. I chose to suffer. This was because I was keeping my self-disconnected from Ceba's and Baby's spirits. Once I could see this, I was able open myself to feeling all my grief. I felt a deep sense of joy in the process of feeling the pain. It was pleasure in the renewed connection with my furry family members and myself. At the end of it all, I realized the truth of the experience. I had done my best to create a safe space for my furry family members to live in peace and humanely.

Now, let's take a moment to reflect on our emotions and see if we are creating suffering or connecting with them. Your emotions are a powerful entry point. Trust your emotions. These emotions will guide you to the right place to discover who you are.

It's like being able to see the difference between suffering and pain. Finally, you have the equipment. You can now move around your day and see where you are on this spectrum. This will allow you to determine if your emotions are controlling you or letting them run through you. It is important to know the difference between them. This will allow you to recognize where you are and give you the ability to decide how to respond. This clarity is essential if you want to move through your life with confidence.

Many people believe that emotion is a sign that you are out of flow. I disagree. You can be in flow when you are fully present and tuned in to yourself. Once you are able to let go of what is not working for you, your emotions will flow like the wind. The wind will blow again, and it will return at a later time. If you resist it, you will continue to feel the wrathful effects of suffering.

Dealing with Pain

Although no one likes to feel pain, the irony of it is that in order to grow and expand our lives, we must feel it. We can't feel the underlying pain if we don't feel it. That will keep us stuck in the same spot as the pain. Until we feel and let go of it. It's because adults can act and behave like children that there are so many of them. Because they didn't learn how to deal with their emotions, they remained stuck. They end up expressing or acting out that repressed pain in their lives.

This is a story I am familiar with. When our relationship reached deeper levels of intimacy and commitment, I would vent on my exes. Because my younger self was raped, I would rage on them whenever they got too close. Fear and shame were still present in my system. Rage covers shameful spots, and I wasn't sure how to deal.

It is better to feel it right away than waiting for it to get worse. It's easier to feel it in real-time because it will be less difficult to process. This is similar to plaque buildup. If you don't floss every day, you will build up plaque layers that will need more work. And if you wait too long the dentist may have to come out with the big guns. You are giving yourself a gift by allowing yourself to feel and work through pain as it occurs. This is a way to honor yourself. You are telling yourself, "I love and trust you that this is possible." You will be able to focus on the mental work. If you feel bloated, it is impossible to eat anything else.

Trauma can be stored in your body, especially if you are going through it alone. When I was young, I didn't know I was suffering trauma. I didn't have the language or understanding to describe what was happening inside me. I knew that I wanted to go away. I have used alcohol, food, drugs, relationships, and, most importantly, my addictions to suffering and drama for years to protect me from my deepest feelings.

Because I wasn't taught how to process emotions, I didn't know how I could process them. This is not something schools teach. This is not something most parents are able to do. It's normal to have suppressed emotions and layers of memories. We can now feel these emotions as adults. It's up to you to create space for yourself to feel compassion and stillness. You need to find stillness in order to feel, especially when you are constantly busy with your life and your mind.

My personality was a mix of being extremely emotionally intelligent due to my empathy and being emotionally out of control due to my inability connect with the parts that needed love. It was only after I quit using my numbing drugs that I was able feel fully and be honest with myself.

Food, social media and work are all common numbing factors. The most overlooked is the addiction to drama and suffering. Because most people are unable to see that they are attached, it is very effective in numbing. You are invited to identify the numbing agents in your life and to let go of them. Watch what emotions you feel as a result of this work. This is why you need a numbing agent. It will keep you from feeling.

It's like releasing your shame and letting go of your inner child. Let's take a look at that for a second. Can you see her? You have been keeping her in a cage for a long time and now you are able to take her out of the dark dungeon-like place, unlock the door and let her go. She will initially be scared and confused about the world outside her cage. As you hold her and show love, she will begin to relax and heal. This is how I felt when I realized that I was neglecting my inner child. It was only after I had reconnected with her that I was able nourish her in the way she needed for so many years. The relationship was built on trust and mutual respect. Because time doesn't go by quickly, your inner child will feel safe and loved.

Shame is a major problem in this country as well as the rest of the world. We, collectively, don't want to get too close to shame. As though shame is something that can be shared with others, we act as if it does. They might avoid us out of fear that they will get lost in the darkness. But the truth is, you can't escape the limbo state that comes with suffering if that happens.

To heal shame, one must go to the depths of your being, where there is no compassion. Then, forgive yourself. Shame cannot live where compassion lives.

Being with Your Emotions Ritual

- It all begins with noticing when an emotional entry point is activated – an emotion starts to bubble up. You feel some sadness arising - or loneliness, or irritation. When you identify that this is happening, create space with a clear and loving intention of healing.
- Go to a quiet place that feels safe, even if that's the bathroom stall at work. Be courageous by giving yourself permission to feel what's coming up for you and surrender to the experience. Be kind to yourself if fears arise or loud voices enter your mind. It's as if you are holding a baby in your arms – it's that sacred of an experience, even if it's for five minutes on the Q train. You are that sacred. When we create this type of space, it already starts the process of healing because loving attention is being put on healing.
- Whether you're standing or sitting, begin by closing your eyes and get in your body by taking three deep breaths into your lower abdomen and feel the breath move through you. Then be still and be in the silence and presence of the moment and feel what is arising in you.
- Are emotions bubbling up? Are childhood memories entering into your visions? Do you hear words popping in? Whatever

is coming up, put your soft attention onto it with an energy of curiosity.

- Allow whatever it is to guide you to the next thing that wants to arise. Perhaps it's another emotion or another memory. It's as if you're on a ride. Don't force it. Surrender to it. Be with it. You may feel an urge to distract yourself, but just gently bring yourself back to the emotions that are wanting attention.
- Tears may fall or not. Be compassionate with yourself however you react to what arises. Hold space for yourself as if you were holding space for your dearest friend or family member.
- Once you feel complete, put both of your hands on your heart and put your attention on your heart space. Thank your heart for being so open and so brave during this experience and express whatever else wants to be shared with your heart. And tell your heart that you will come back to this space whenever your heart needs you.
- Then take three deeps breaths to reconnect with your body. Take a moment to thank the Universe, your ancestors, and loved ones on the other side for all of their love, holding, and guidance. And then slowly open your eyes.
- Journal about your experience so you can digest what just happened. Insights, images, words, feelings, memories. Write freely without too much thought. Let your hands do the writing. Then take your time transitioning into what you need to do next.

When you feel more at ease with yourself, you will know you have a deeper relationship with your heart space. You'll feel more at ease with your emotions, and you will crave forgiveness and presence. You'll be able to give yourself exquisite attention and love, and you will notice when you aren't. You'll be able be completely honest with yourself about the things you've been keeping from others. You will learn to slow down, find your own pace and respect it. While you won't expect others to take good care of your needs, they will show their appreciation when they do.

Forgiveness

Sometimes we feel our emotions, but still can't forgive ourselves. Women who hide behind their weight and aren't open to forgiveness are just as guilty as anyone else. They hold on to so much resentment. That's part the weight you need to let go of in order to get rid of your body armor.

Since I was a child, I have held grudges against other people. I was full of resentment. The day I realized that my resentment was directed at me, that's when I began to forgive. I felt the pain I had caused my entire life. My lack of self-forgiveness was affecting my relationships and me. Because the way we feel about ourselves is projected onto the world, it was difficult to see. It's a direct correlation - no exceptions. Everybody is my mirror, and an entry point to my power.

My acupuncture practice was not only about supporting my patients on their journeys, but also my own growth. They reflected back to me what I needed to see in my own life. Six years ago, I was dealing with a patient who would often come in feeling overwhelmed by her spinning mind. Because I wasn't having the impact I wanted, I felt stressed every time I saw her. She didn't appreciate my suggestions and felt insecure. I was unsure of my abilities to allow for growth and self-reflection in order to be a better person. Then, I realized that I was projecting my expectations of success onto her and was disappointed in her progress. This was all about me and my feelings of insufficient and the need to help others. Unknowingly, she reflected my spinning mind and inability of being present with what was going on at the time. It was both empowering and humble to see myself in my reflections and projections. This experience changed my entire acupuncture practice as well as how I hold space to my patients. In a split second, I can tell if my ego wants to control me or if it's really about them.

A whole new world is possible if we are open to seeing things from different perspectives. You will see that what you think or say about others is also what you think about yourself. This requires an open mind and a shift of perspective. However, if we pay attention to how we think about others, we can have a tremendous opportunity to reach deeper into our power.

To forgive, we must be able to accept responsibility for our actions and not pass it onto others. We can see the lines in our boundaries. This is your garden. I am your garden.

When we see clearly our boundaries, we can direct our attention away from ourselves and instead focus it on us. We can choose to be brutally honest about how we have hurt others and ourselves. We choose to let go of all the unkind ways we have treated others. We create a list of people who have hurt us, including ourselves. Then we admit to the unkind things we did and then we direct our loving energy towards them/us.

Forgiveness Ritual

- Make a list of all the people you are resentful toward or are not on good terms with.
- One at a time, write down why you are resentful toward each one of them.
- Write down what part you played in each circumstance. The thoughts and behaviors that contributed to the disconnection.

- Write down what you could have done instead.
- Ask yourself if it is possible to forgive them.

- Take a moment to ask yourself if you are willing to forgive yourself.
- Sit with the emotions arising and see if you can feel some love bubbling up in you.
- Burn the paper and say out loud, "I forgive you" and "I forgive myself".
- When you feel complete, thank yourself for being so courageous in this act of releasing blame.

Forgiveness is an effective medicine for any shame, anger, guilt. Although you may not be aware of it right away if your tendency is to numb yourself or distract from the pain, there are usually feelings of guilt and blame. If we can be present with our pain, there is more room for blame to emerge. It's much easier to place blame on others when you see the fault. Take a look at the things you blame others for and use it as a guideline to seeing yourself in the mirror. I often see that I have resentment toward myself. However, I have displaced my resentment onto others. Because of this, I am a strong believer in self-forgiveness. When we can do this, it will be easier to forgive others. It is more efficient to get to the root of a weed than to keep cutting the branches.

Self-forgiveness seems to be the best way to build a close relationship with yourself. Are you judging your emotional eating or being kind to yourself? You must forgive yourself for any situation where you have been unkind to your self, whether it is emotionally eating after a stressful day or yelling at someone afterwards.

Guilt is not an emotion, but a state in your mind. Your ego is telling you you have done something wrong. This is a set of thoughts that lead you to a path of suffering and rumination. It's interesting to note that your ego can tell your mind that you did something wrong for any reason, even if it is completely fabricated by your imagination. You don't get called back by someone. Instead, you tell yourself a story about what you did wrong and feel guilty. They are simply busy working on a project. When you add food to the mix, or if you don't exercise, it creates a false narrative that you aren't doing it right. Your mind believes it should be done in one way, the "right". Because your perspective is narrow and narrow like a tunnel, there's only one choice and you're completely committed to it, guilt can occur.

This was me. My world was ruled by guilt. I made up stories after stories that weren't true. As a result, my mind was filled with drama and I felt guilty for countless hours.

We can forgive ourselves and use that experience to learn more about ourselves. We can consciously examine what is happening beneath the surface to question our feelings about it.

It is important to forgive yourself for past or present mistakes, big and small, and it will increase our ability to love and accept ourselves. We can be kind and compassionate towards ourselves, even in situations where we hold onto guilt, and we can then extend that compassion to others, no matter if it is a stranger cutting you off at the roadside or someone we love who has done something deeply hurtful.

Forgiveness is for you because it liberates you. It frees you from the prison you have made for yourself.

— Louise Hay

Embodiment

This is the Ph.D. in honoring emotions and being so right about how you feel. It's like embracing all of it. This ritual can be repeated several times before you feel comfortable with it. Trust your gut instincts.

Embodiment is when you can be in touch with your emotions. Let them guide your body to express your feelings. This requires deep listening to your emotions and connecting with your body.

This is the same process as the above ritual, but there are two additional steps. You may feel the urge to move your body while you're feeling whatever is coming up in you. You can listen to music that will help you get the juices flowing if you are having trouble getting your thoughts moving.

Let go of your thoughts and let the emotions lead you to express or move whatever emotion you desire. It's possible to feel strange. This is a sign that you are doing it right. Allow yourself to be open to your emotions. Your facial expressions, bodily movements and voice are yours to express. Think of yourself as a child, free from cultural expectations. You can be free to express your emotions, cry, scream, curse or stomp about, punch the couch, or do interpretive dances. Perfection is what comes out of you. Once you feel complete, you can move your hips around in circles before you perform the closing hands on the heart portion. Feel the juiciness in your body and your 'turn-on'.

This is how I used the ritual to continue my grieving process after the death of my pet. While I was writing the first draft, I felt a slight sadness rise as I sat in my living room. But, as I concentrated my attention, it grew. I just sat there with it. I then heard an inner voice tell me to move my body. I stood up and allowed my body to do what it wanted. I danced, crouched down and moaned in pain. I also wiggled my arms in the air, as if asking for help from the Universe. I simply listened to my body, one moment at a time. Then, suddenly, I stopped. I stood in my living room, my hands covering my heart, and tears began to pour out of my eyes. Although it was not graceful or beautiful, it was exactly what I felt that moment.

This was a sacred act in love. This was a way for me to honor my grief and the human journey. We ignore the human condition and deny it any expression. When we choose to embrace the beauty of our emotions, we transform our pain into love. This increases our capacity to receive love and abundance in life. It increases the love we can offer. It increases our gratitude for all aspects of life. You can fill your cup.

CHAPTER 7

Rewiring Your Brain (The Mental Realm)

"Don't believe everything that you think."

— Byron Katie

It's a new world when you see clearly. No veil. No matrix. No kidding. It is tricky to be egoistic and can do many things.

Anything to brainwash you, convince you of its lies and sabotage your mind. You are made to believe that you are not worthy or loved, and it is true. Many people live their lives on worn-out identities that no longer serve their needs. They live in 2020, with an outdated IBM computer. It is time to upgrade your hard disk!

Maybe you've forgotten that your body, which is unique and beautiful, is perfect. You are the only one in this world who has ever come even close to being like you. You will be the only person in the future who is even close to you. Are you aware that anything in your life, even your physical body, could and would change if you allowed yourself to see things differently?

Your thoughts can influence how your brain thinks and affect how you feel about yourself and your life. You will eventually start to believe the negative thoughts you have about yourself, your body, money, relationships, and family. You can rewire your brain so that it believes new thoughts and beliefs. Your beliefs create your life. Which lens or filter do you use? You can find out what lens or filter you are using by simply observing your reality right now. Listen and be still.

Are you able to control your mind or are you more comfortable in victim consciousness? It is easy to become complacent in a chaotic mind, especially if that's your normal state. You probably don't know what it's like to feel calm and peaceful if you haven't been taught how to focus your mind. If you don't know what you're missing, you won't know what's possible.

Addicted to Suffering

It was almost like I had woken up from a bad dream to realize that I was suffering from an addiction to suffering. It was like Neo waking up in reality after taking the red pill. It was quite shocking to realize how much drama I created in my life and my mind in order to not live fully and be present. It was at first humbling, because it was so hard to believe that it took me so much time to see it. It was right in front my face. How could I have missed it? It was obvious when I looked back: I was creating drama all the time. I could not stop worrying about what others thought of me, what was wrong about me, blahblahblah. This is what happens when you become addicted to something. It's impossible to see beyond that addiction. You only want the next hit. I was unable to take full control of my life and mind because of those hits. I was unable to be in control of my life and mind. I was unable to radiate my light and it kept me in hiding.

It was then that I realized my addiction and took responsibility for it. It was easy to see when I was being manipulated by my temptress ego. I chose to stop going down this path because my joy, pleasure, and peace were greater than my outworn need for suffering. This became easier as I realized how important my peace of mind was and refused to let go.

After I had gotten out of my self-inflicted matrix, it was time to quit my old M.O. There were no withdrawal symptoms. Nope! Nope! Instead, I felt more in control and lighter than ever before. It was a miracle and a game-changer.

Can you see why you are so addicted to drama and suffering? Take a closer look.

Ego Training

Dog trainer was one of many jobs that I have had in my life. It is best to tell a dog to stop doing something negative while they are thinking about it. It is second-most effective to give the command while the dog is actually doing the act. The last is when the target behavior is already taking place.

To be a good trainer, you need to always be one step ahead. Potty training your dog requires that you are always aware of them. Ceba was just a puppy when I was able to tell her when she was going to potty. I can remember the way she began looking around, sniffing and walking. I became more adept at catching her before she tried to go potty indoors.

Everyone who had the opportunity to work with Ceba mentioned how well-trained she was. Cesar Millan, Dog Whisperer, explains that it's important to love, calm and be assertive.

Imagine your ego as a dog. You must train your ego to be calm and assertive when it's acting out. It will be a waste of time to punish the ego for its unwanted behavior. How many people will blame their dog for unwanted behavior? The same goes for their egos. It's the responsibility of the individual to be the calm, assertive, loving alpha. The ego does what it does. It is you who must be one step ahead, looking at it.

Cesar's quote is my favorite because it illustrates the nature and power of the ego. "If you only give eighty percent leadership, then your dog will give eighty percent following." He will take over the show the remaining twenty percent. You should give your dog every opportunity to lead you.

You will eventually be able, with practice, to move ahead of your ego. This will allow you to avoid any self-destructive behaviors. You will eventually learn to love yourself and set firm boundaries.

Martyr Story and Boundaries

Everything is a mirror. Every situation and person is a mirror of ourselves. Everything is a reflection on who we are or what we're thinking or going through. This new lens allows you to see everything through a different lens.

My observation has shown that many women live a martyr story. This is why I believe women conceal their weight. It's a great way to hide. It doesn't mean you have to be a martyr. If you don't achieve what you want, you can blame others. It is possible to live a lie of being "good". Giving to others can be more comfortable than giving to yourself. It can feel safer to give to others than it does to think about yourself. You feel safer putting yourself on a pedestal and claiming to be better than others. This makes it easier to judge others and keeps you from the intimacy and connection you so desperately want. If you don't receive what you expect, you close your heart. How you convince yourself that you are worthy and loved by others, or through people-pleasing, will determine your existence.

Low self-worth and low self-esteem can make you appear like you have it all and are doing well because you are selfless. One of my clients stated, "Being selfless is actually having less of oneself." This trick story is tricky because it convinces people that you are creating value. But in reality, your energy tank and resentment tanks are full.

Boundaries are the antidote to martyrdom. It is possible that you are influenced by the martyr story and your boundaries may be fuzzy at best. It is possible that you don't even know where the line is. It is possible that you don't know what to say "yes" or "no".

This is a good place to start. Ask yourself what it would be like to make a conscious decision to live your life for yourself. What would it look like to live your life without being dictated by others? Maybe it was your parents' expectations when you were young. Or maybe it was your partner's or your community's or society's expectations. There is no better time than now to make a commitment. Waiting will make you resentful and prevent you from living the life that you want for X number of days, weeks, years, decades, or decades.

It will be easier to establish loving, yet firm boundaries with your self and your ego. It will be easier to establish loving, yet firm boundaries with your ego.

Another mirror is the connection between boundaries with yourself and others. In acupuncture school, I was taught two terms: visceral–somatic and somatic–visceral. This means that muscle tightness around your abdomen can be caused by an internal problem such as chronic digestion problems. Digestive issues can also be caused by muscle tightness around your abdomen. There is no disconnect. External effects have internal effects and vice versa. Micro macro. Yin yang.

It is important to know where your line is. You have your garden, and I have mine. We often find ourselves in the same place, sometimes even sharing our gardens. What about our garden? These are the actions of martyrs, who believe they are helping the other person.

You can direct your attention inward when you are able to clearly see the line. It's like an arrow to me. My arrow was always going outwards for most of my life. What can I do? What can I do? What do they think about me? They are all up in their business. You are trying to be a mind reader. When you are aware of your limits and can see what is happening, you can pivot and turn that arrow towards yourself to do the work that brings you happiness and peace. You can't control the world outside. This is a fact you are seeing over and over. The truth is that you won't be able get into the heads of others and you won't be able change them. This is insane, and it's what I did for the majority of my life.

Boundary Research Ritual

This exercise is designed to help you develop your self-integrity. It will open up entry points for you and give you many opportunities to complete the work.

You can create a container that will both honor your "yes" and your "no". Containers are similar to making a structure that has "rules". A container supports research by providing a safe environment. You can choose a time period, such as a week, a months, or a year. It was a good way to honor myself. I did it for several months. You can decide if you want to be more focused on one area of your life, or all areas. You can also create other "rules" that you feel good about.

When someone asks for something or asks for your permission to do something, STOP and ask yourself "Do I want to do this?" Then let your body answer. Most times you will know the answer immediately. This exercise doesn't require your logical mind. Your answer is the first one that appears. If you don't answer YES, you are a no.

If you are unsure of your answer, or feel uncomfortable sharing the truth, you can be your own answer. After you've had a chance to think about the request, let the requestor know you'll get back to them with an explanation. You should take the time to reflect on your feelings and not feel pressured to respond immediately. People who don't know how to set boundaries and are afraid of saying no will feel pressured to answer every request immediately. Take your time. There is no death.

If you get a "no", don't be surprised. Simply respond "no, thankyou." There is no need to make excuses. You have control over your life, your time, and your energy. Without having to explain, you can do what you wish with it. For a time, it will feel uncomfortable but you will soon start to feel a sense of freedom. You won't be a slave to people-pleasing any longer. If you want to fluff your response, notice. It will be obvious very quickly how much you lack boundaries and have just gone along because.

This is the best part. If you are a yes, it will be something you really enjoy and you will be fully present. You'll start to notice how much time you spent on things you didn't want to do.

These situations require that you eliminate the words ok and fine from your vocabulary. These words are a sign of lack of ownership and not being able to do what you want. Do you answer yes or no?

Body Beliefs

Limiting beliefs about the body can be either covert or explicit. This is true regardless of whether they are based on social media or a result from sexual abuse or assault. The insidious virus is the covert version. Many women believe the same thing - that being thin is necessary to look attractive and sexy. This false message can be drilled into our heads by so many external sources that we might not even know it. These limiting beliefs can become a virus that causes body shame and self-hate over time.

One of my clients discovered that she had been obsessive about losing weight since she was little. She wanted to look like "skinny girls". She felt different than her peers and the media's portrayal of women. People feel different when they feel like an "outsider".

Her mother wanted her to be thin, too. Limiting beliefs can be passed down from one generation to the next until someone changes their mind and questions them. She now realizes she wasn't fat, even though she believed she was. When she was eight years of age, her body dysmorphia and body shame were started. This is a common belief that has spread to the masses, according to all the feedback I have received from women.

However, if a woman is sexually abused, it can be a clear indication of her body shame beliefs. This happens when a woman feels guilty for the abuse, even though it wasn't her fault. Another reason could be that she felt responsible for the abuse and was forced to create body armor. She used the clear information she received from her experience to make a direct correlation with how her body feels.

Limiting beliefs don't discriminate. They can be either overt or covert. If a belief persists for many years without intervention, it will continue to feed on the beliefs and grow like a parasite.

The Saboteur

As I gained more awareness about my upper limits, and my sabotaging behavior, I began to identify my saboteur. This allowed me to draw a line between who I was and what my ego wanted me to believe I was. I realized that my saboteur was actually the young, fearful parts of me. It was the survival mode part of me that just wanted to be protected at all costs. My eight-year old self appeared as I got to know her.

She was both adorable and terrifying at the same moment. She would run amok, spy on me from the corner, waiting for the right moment to attack. I saw her innocent, scared little girl and decided to love her just as she was. I placed her at the child's table, along with her friends and a blanket. She felt at ease there. Every time she would act out, I would try to find a way for me to calm her down and give her a sense safety. Sometimes it was cuddling her up in a soft, cozy bed with stuffed animals. Sometimes, I would cuddle with her. My nervous system also relaxed immediately.

Because I was able separate her from me, it was successful. It was her fear that was the problem, and not her. I was able see her with a

compassionate heart.

It is not about denying the thoughts or ego, but about accepting that it is what the ego does. It doesn't matter what it is. It's just how we are wired as humans. You can see it from a distance if you stop taking it personally. You realize that you have the power to change the dynamic and you start using it every day.

Tantrum Love Ritual

Begin by looking at the most repetitive, most negative thoughts. These are the ones that sound like a broken record. Imagine yourself as a young child when you feel fearful or insecure. Get to know her. What are her clothes? What is her facial expression like? What's her facial expression?

Imagine her throwing a fit while uttering the same repetitive thoughts over and over again. Take a look at her with compassionate, motherly eyes. Do you see her in pain? She just needs your love. Do you want to open your heart to her? Now, create a scene in which you love her. What would you want as a child? What do you think she is looking for? You can give her the attention and love that she needs. Relax her nervous system.

Make sure you feel complete together and tell her that you love her.

Questioning and Visualizing

You might be very curious, but are you limiting your curiosity to the areas you feel comfortable and confident in? Do you ask questions that are based on a limited belief? What if you asked questions that were totally out of your box?

One participant knew she was carrying a martyr story. It was all she knew. Although her awareness was beyond comprehension, she carried the martyr story with pride. She was asking the wrong questions, and she kept suffering. Her life changed dramatically when she started asking herself "If I dare to do things differently, how would it look like?" It was possible for her to attend exercises classes, where she had felt guilty about leaving her children with a nanny. After twenty years of being together, she was able ask her husband for the kind of sensual touch that she wanted.

Curiosity doesn't mean asking questions. However, that can be a powerful tool. It is important to look at the world with wonder and be amazed by people and the world around you.

We often make statements that are not facts, instead of asking questions. It can help us shift from our tunnel vision to see other options and perspectives by asking questions. You can rewire your brain by adding visualization to the mix. Although neuroplasticity is real, it's not possible to achieve without practice. Your mind will continue on the same path as it has always been if you don't practice. It's like watching Groundhog Day. People use imagination to discredit themselves and others instead of being constructive. They will imagine the worst things that have ever happened, instead of seeing the potential.

People are asking the wrong questions, because they are focused on "Why?". The second problem is that "Why?" can be a distraction and lead to a lot of wrong questions. "Why?" is about the past. It makes you think about your problems, and it is not like feeling emotions when an entry point activation occurs. It's like a cat following their tail. You will keep spinning in the exact same place. These are the most powerful questions. They open up your mind to possibilities in areas that you've never considered. This opens up your brain to new possibilities and allows you to see the world through visualization. You can feel it like you are there. You can't see the possibilities if you don't believe it is possible. You wouldn't crave chocolate if you hadn't heard of it.

The Two Versions of You Ritual

This list contains powerful questions that you can use for this ritual. Or, you can make your own. The question can be asked in relation to a particular situation in your life.

- How would life look and feel if I dared to do things I desired?
- What would happen if I let go of this resentment? How would I feel? How would life be different?
- How would life change if I stopped putting everyone else before me? How would I feel?
- What would happen if I trusted the Universe?
- What would my life look like if I stopped hiding?
-
- What would my life look like if I let go of my fear fat suit?
- What would your life look like if you chose me first?

What would my thoughts and beliefs make me feel? How would I treat others?

- What if I choose to see this situation differently?

Close your eyes and find a quiet, private place to sit. To get in touch with the present moment and your body, take three deep breaths. Two identical images of yourself are placed next to one another. The left image is your current self, who is currently suffering from a specific situation. The right image is your future self who can see possibilities. It is believed that the left-most version of yourself is how you have lived your life with a belief that has caused suffering, while the right-most version is who you are.

Ask one of these questions in the negative side of your body and the other in the positive side of your body. Each version of the question should be asked one at a time. Example: Ask the first question, "How would my life look and feel if it was possible to do what I wanted?" The negative question is "How would my life look and feel if I didn't dare do the things I want?"

Each version of yourself should feel the emotion that is triggered by the question. Images will come to mind when you ask the question. Let them explore the world with curiosity and let them come up with their own answers.

Now, compare them. Visualize the differences in their lives and how they feel. Visualize your life as if it were an action movie. You are the star actor. Do not force the images. It's okay to take it in. You are in control of your beliefs and their impact on your life.

Take three deep, slow breaths when you feel complete. You can take a moment to express gratitude to the Universe, your ancestors and all loved ones on the other side. Slowly open your eyes. Keep a journal about what you have experienced to help you process it. Insights, images, words, feelings, memories. You can write freely and without thinking. Allow your fingers to do the writing. Take your time to decide what next step you should take.

This mediation has the advantage of allowing you to see how much control and power you have over your life. You can also learn to say no to your ego whenever it pleases you. You will see that it is important to focus your attention on something else than what you have been thinking and believing.

Remember to do The Work by Byron Katie. The system is simple and uses four questions. It also includes a turn-around process that will help you with your belief inquiry.

"If you sacrifice yourself for others, you are making them a thief. They are stealing what you need.

don't even know it."

— Iyanla Vanzant

CHAPTER 8

The Body Knows (The Physical Realm)

"Your body has more wisdom than your deepest philosophies."

Friedrich Nietzche It is a sacred act of love to your body. But what does it mean? It is about accepting your body, listening to its messages, taking care of it and trusting them.

Weight loss is a spiritual practice. For women who have done a lot of emotional and spiritual work it can also be the final frontier. The practice of being present to your body is profoundly spiritual. If you can't love and care about your temple in a way it is, respecting its perfection, then you are telling your ultimate creator, source of energy, that your trust in them, the laws, or yourself is lacking.

From all my explorations into the healing realms, I found that the journey of releasing my weight was the most profound. It was my last frontier and required me to cultivate intimacy with myself. Otherwise, the weight release will not stick.

Because it reminded of my own inequalities, I hated being overweight. I felt tired all the time and didn't have the energy or motivation to do the things I wanted. I was a lonely couch potato living in a fantasy world of hoping and wishing that my dreams would come true, but I didn't want to do anything. If you allow magic thinking to take control of your life, it can. I wanted to lose weight, but I wasn't willing to put in the effort to achieve it. Now, I see that my weight-loss journey was a gift.

This has allowed me to connect with the divine in a way I don't know how I would have done without it. Our connection to the source energy grows when we can alchemize our deepest fears, pains, and transform them into something positive.

This possibility is possible because of your newly acquired intuition. Your intuition will become more clear and louder as you continue to do this work. This will allow you to tap into an all-knowing power. This level of trust and surrender will bring you peace. You will be able connect to the unseen world.

My traumas made me a prisoner in my own body. It was almost dissociating from me. It was a way of life that I believed was normal. I didn't know I was living beyond my body. Only sex was a clue. I would check out myself after sex, and then I would need to bring myself back into the present. When I felt anxious, I would dissociate. Because this was my norm, I didn't realize I was so disconnected with my body. You may not realize what you are missing if you have lived a certain lifestyle for most of your adult life. Embodiment practices were the only way I was able to feel a connection with my body.

To cultivate a deeper connection with your body, you must feel the sensations within. I see sensations as little fairies who live within me. They can be powerful entry points to a magical world of healing and discovery. As with all entrance points, the sensations can guide you into subconscious spaces that hold information that can help you be free.

Identifying Sensations

My patients are always encouraged to listen to their bodies. But what does this mean? If you don't have a relationship, how can you tell what your body wants to say? This chapter aims to help you develop a close relationship with your body in order to listen to its endless wisdom. You must first practice feeling. You will feel sensations in your body, just as you do when you connect to your emotions. One of the reasons I love acupuncture is that it allows you to feel sensations in your body. A client may feel various sensations during an acupuncture session, such as throbbing, heaviness and waves of energy moving through the body. It takes practice to recognize and feel sensations.

It is common for people to assume that sensations mean what they are conditioned to believe. You may believe that a racing heart is a sign of anxiety, but it could also be a sign you are excited. Our pre-conditioned perceptions of sensations lead us to react on them with our minds. What if you felt the sensation and didn't make any assumptions about what it meant? This is mindfulness.

This is the same practice you have been doing with your emotions, your thoughts and now with your body.

Body Scan Ritual

This ritual can be used if you feel an intense sensation such as a sharp pain, or if you don't feel any sensations and want to get in touch with someone.

In a quiet and private space, sit down. Three deep, slow breaths are enough to connect you with your body. Pay attention to your feet and feel for any sensations. Next, slowly work your way up the body one part at a while until you reach the top.

Slow down so that you can feel all sensations.

Focus your attention on a sensation you are experiencing.

It is important to feel it, not try to control or change it. Be with it. It might dissipate, or it could not. It could move, or it might not. It might change in quality or temperature, or it may not. Be with it. Then, move on to the next part of your body.

Images may spontaneously appear. A message may be heard. It is possible to feel a certain feeling, or not. You may notice a certain feeling if you do or not, but it is important to remain curious.

You can follow the sensation, just like a sled. Be present for any memories or emotions that arise. As described in the chapter on the emotional realm, allow yourself to be present.

The sensation can be asked a question such as "What do you want me know?" Let the answer come. Listen to what your body has to say. It doesn't always have a message. This is a way to build a relationship with your body. It takes time to feel safe and comfortable enough to share your feelings with someone new, just like with a lover or friend. Your body deserves love and kindness.

Take three deep, slow breaths when you feel complete. You can take a moment to express gratitude to the Universe, your ancestors and all loved ones on the other side. Slowly open your eyes. Keep a journal about what you have experienced to help you process it. Insights, images, words, feelings, memories. You can write freely and without thinking. Allow your fingers to do the writing. Take your time to decide what next step you should take.

You will allow your body to express itself just as you do with your emotions or your thoughts. All you have to do now is to listen and feel.

Your relationship with your body will grow by allowing it to feel what it wants without you dictating it.

Start by relaxing in stillness and quiet. Next, do a body scan. Begin by focusing your attention on your feet. Feel them. Next, move your focus up the body, slowly moving up your hips, torso and neck. Every part of your body has its own voice. Seek out the sensations and be curious.

You will soon feel sensations everywhere you go, with a lot of people, and wherever you want. It all comes down to cultivating your attention. You will feel more connected to your sensations and be able to sense sensations in situations you didn't know existed.

Whether you have intense sensations or not, it's a great practice to pay attention to them throughout the day. Doing check-ins will shift your relationship with your body. You can sit at your desk at work, close your eyes, start your body scan, and take note of what you're feeling. Perhaps your toes feel cold; there's some subtle tingling in your thighs; your low back feels tight and achy; your stomach feels warm; your right index fingertip has an electric sensation; your chest feels heavy; and your forehead is achy.

This is not uncommon to have all these different sensations happening at one time. It takes time and practice to identify them and learn how to express these sensations into words.

Sensations are complex and are made up of different aspects. Here's a guideline that will help you to identify them and give language to them:

- Intensity: very subtle to very extreme and everything in between.
- Qualities: temperature-based (hot, warm, cold), electricity, tingles, sharpness, aches, heaviness, burning, pinching, tight, soft, numbness, etc.
- Temperature: cold, warm, hot, chilly
- Duration: range from a quick moment to long-lasting.
- Location: anywhere in the body.

Sensations can give us messages about what our physical and emotional bodies need. They are a guide if we let them be. Once you practice listening to your body, you will eventually be able to have a conversation with it. You will learn to interpret the sensations with your intuition, not your mind.

A week after I broke up with my ex, I had an accident that tore my shoulder labrum. It was the most intense sensation I had ever experienced. After the initial frustration that this happened, I got clear that it happened because I was feeling so guilty because of my martyrdom story and that I was subconsciously punishing myself. But the thing is, I used this high-intensity sharp sensation in my shoulder to guide me through my emotional healing process and my weightreleasing process.

I was forced to slow down because if I didn't, I would feel everything intensely. I had to take exquisite care of myself so I could heal. I had to put all of the attention on self-care versus my guilt. The pain became my daily moment-to-moment meditation. It kept bringing me back to my body over and over. It was such a gift.

It's also a reminder that injuries don't need to be a roadblock in our weight-releasing journey because this is the time when I released forty pounds. So, no excuses when it comes to injuries. I chose exercises that didn't bother my arm like jogging and jumping on my trampoline. If the desire is there, anything is possible.

Most of the time, people are annoyed by the sensations in their bodies and just want to get rid of them. You have a stomachache, and you just take medicine to get rid of the discomfort, but did you take a moment to ask your stomach what it needs? What's the underlying root issue that needs attention here? Band-Aids only last so long. What if we asked what medicine we really need right now and were able to listen to what our bodies tell us?

I have had many powerful experiences where a sensation has brought me deeper into healing. I recall a specific moment during another breakup: I was triggered in this particular moment and thought that I was being used for sex. I went home, laid in my bed, and all of a sudden, I felt a strong ache in my chest, and my heart started beating faster. Perhaps someone else would have labeled it anxiety and from that label would have actually created an anxiety attack. But I was clear that it was just sensation, and it was trying to tell me something.

I closed my eyes and allowed myself to sink into it. Then all of a sudden, the sensation took me to a memory of my first rape. I was brought back to the exact moment where he was penetrating me. I looked in his eyes and felt the pain inside of him. I was overcome by compassion for this person who had hurt me. Then the sensation moved down to my lower abdomen, feeling heavy and thick. I was then brought to a recent memory of the man I had just broken up with and was able to feel that same level of compassion for him, even though just moments before, I was categorizing him as a perpetrator. It felt like a trip, but I was completely sober.

This is what's possible when we feel. Sensations are like sleds. They can lead us to these powerful entry points of healing if you surrender to them.

The Yang Portal

CHAPTER 9

Turn Your Body ON

"Within my body are all the sacred places of the world, and the most profound pilgrimage I can ever make is within my own body."

— Saraha

Dancing

Dancing is a surefire way of getting in your body and turning on. If you are stuck in your head and need a reset, put on your favorite jams and let the music move you. I'm guessing pretty much everyone has experienced the power of dancing. Music has such a powerful effect on your emotional state, imagine what happens when you pair it with dancing like there's no tomorrow, and when you let your moves be full of heart.

You can dance every morning as soon as you wake up to get your juices moving, or you can dance once every hour while at work. Perhaps you're doing your taxes and need to get turned on to keep you from procrastinating. That's what I did. I literally filed for an extension every year for as long as I could remember, but when I used dancing as a tool to get turned on, I was able to file my taxes not only on time, but early! Miracles happen when we are tapped into the electricity that is available to us at any moment; even tax miracles!

Add a mirror to get even more connected to yourself. Witness your joy and love bursting out of you and get even more turned on. You have this amazing body that you were born into and it's here to live life and to be in pleasure. Flirt with yourself. Dance sensually. Dance like a wild woman. However your body wants to move, do it.

Dancing Ritual

Turn on whatever song that makes you feel whatever emotion you're feeling or desire to feel. And dance like no one's watching. Get into it. Feel your energy rise as you let any heaviness or worries that are present wash away. Check yourself out in the mirror. Smile at yourself. Circle those hips! However your body wants to move, just do it. She knows what she wants so follow her lead. Feel the elation and electricity rise. This is you in all of your expressive glory. Don't hold back. This moment is all for you. Feel the turn-on that lives in you. You were made for this.

When you feel complete, take a moment to thank your beautiful body, your loved ones on the other side, and your higher power for holding space for this alchemical journey.

Mirror Work

Another way of cultivating a loving and intimate relationship with your body is to see the beauty of it, as it is. Do you ever look at yourself naked in a full-length mirror? Seeing yourself exactly as you are, with no judgment, is a game-changer.

When we transform what was once negative in our minds to something beautiful, anything is possible. Our bodies truly become a work of art, whether we are overweight or not. Mirror work is powerful because you get to be with yourself in a way that is open and connected. Normally when we look in the mirror, it's prepping how we want to be seen in the world like when we do our make-up or hair or even practical reasons, like flossing our teeth. But how often do you look at yourself to say how much you love you or tell yourself how beautiful you are? Mirror work allows us to see us as we are and learn full acceptance, approval, and love of self.

Mirror Work Ritual

Start by eye-gazing with yourself close to the mirror. Connect with yourself. Look at yourself as if you were your lover, with loving, affectionate eyes. Look so deeply that you can feel your own soul.

Once you feel that loving connection, step back and take a look at your entire body, naked in all of its glory. You may feel twinges of judgments or full-on self-hatred. Whatever arises is okay. Just notice what your thoughts are and make a note of it. Take a deep breath and then look at yourself again with soft eyes (that means to relax your eyes so they're kind of in a dreamy state, like half-way closed).

Look at the part of your body that you love the most and gaze at it with affection. Tell yourself, in your mind or out loud, how much you love it and thank it for all it has done for you while touching it lovingly. If it's your legs, you can say something like, "I love you. Thank you for being so strong, keeping me rooted, and taking me wherever I've needed to go."

Then go to a part of your body you have judgments about. Still with a soft, loving gaze, touch it and caress it while you thank it and tell it you love it. If it's your stomach, you could say, "I love you. Thank you for protecting my sex organs all these years. I needed this layer of fat to feel safe, and I appreciate you for honoring my need for safety."

Make sure to include scars, stretch marks, and cellulite on your list of things to put loving attention on. This will impact you more than you can ever imagine.

If you can't find any gratitude yet, just caress it with love. Then try next time to find the words. Start off with one part you love and one part you don't love. Then you can increase these based on how you feel. I recommend doing this daily for about five to ten minutes first thing in the morning or before bed.

When you feel complete, take a moment to thank your reflection, your loved ones on the other side, and your higher power for holding space for this transformative experience.

After I lost forty pounds, I noticed that I had new stretch marks on my butt, calves, breasts, and upper arms. At first, I freaked and had a moment of disappointment and judgment. My vision of what I thought I wanted disappeared just like that. But as I've shared, entry point activations are gifts because they open the portal into healing. So I used this opportunity to love myself even more.

I did mirror work on my stretch marks every day for a few days, and there was a moment when I looked at them and felt a deep love for them when I saw an image of the rings on a tree. Each ring around a tree represents a year of existence. They are growth rings. I felt this profound sense of love for my growth marks and for how my body has gone through so much over the years and still stood there with so much power and vitality. My growth marks are now an indication of my emotional maturity and physical strength to move through challenging times in my life, not an indication of failure.

Self-Pleasure

I also recommend self-pleasuring as often as you can, not only touching your erogenous zones but also all areas of your body. Perhaps your tummy likes being held, or maybe your thigh likes to be caressed, or perhaps your ear likes a little pinch. Get to know what feels good to you. What sensations do you like? What sensations do you not? Put attention on the parts that you tend to ignore. Rub them, caress them, stroke them.

Your body has been ignored and shamed long enough. You must take a radical step if you want radical self-love. Even if you feel like you're faking it at first, do it anyway, no matter what your ego tries to tell you. Your resistance will demand that you do something else more important, like Netflix. Or perhaps you'll have an urge to emotionally eat in that very moment. These are all perfect because they are signals giving you information, which is telling you about your resistance. Maybe you are afraid and want to check out, but resistances usually arise when we are close to an opening or a breakthrough.

Self-Pleasure Ritual

Create space to be present with yourself, whether in your bedroom, in your office, on the train. Wherever you are, let your fingers and hands explore your body. If in a public space, perhaps using the tip of your finger to slide gently along the top of your hand. If in private, feel free to be as naked or as clothed as you desire.

Be curious and take your time. Go slowly and fully receive your touch.

Touch a spot on your body that you've never put attention on or touch a spot that you have put attention on but now touch it in a new way. How does it feel to the spot being touched? How does it feel to the part doing the touching? Take in this moment and feel how the subtle sensations are turning your body on. Soak in the juiciness that is you. Connect with the deliciousness of your body.

When you feel complete, take a moment to thank your body, your loved ones on the other side, and your higher power for holding space for this sensual experience.

Sweet Talk

How many times have you done the opposite of sweet-talking to yourself? Are you downright mean to yourself about your body? Is it a constant stream of subtle negative internal comments you make to yourself? I dare you to flip this script and start talking to yourself in the loving way that a lover would. Whisper sweet nothings as you caress your soft skin. Use a tone that is generous and loving, and do it often.

Whenever you notice yourself saying unkind things to yourself, it's the perfect time to sweet talk yourself. Or try sweet talking to yourself when you're feeling stressed. Or sweet talk for no other reason than that you just want to love on yourself. You don't even have to have a reason. Do it because it feels good. You deserve to be talked to with kindness, appreciation, and love. Have you ever considered that when you overeat sweet foods, that what you really might be craving is another kind of sweetness altogether? Like many of the practices in this book, sweet-talk may feel weird or uncomfortable at first, but I believe that as you continue to practice, you will find yourself enjoying the playfulness and the pleasure that ensues. Sweet talk will start to feel like home, like you may even exclaim, "How have I not done this all of my life?"

Sweet Talk Ritual

While looking in a mirror with soft eyes, tell yourself how amazing you are. Believe it. Tell yourself that you are beautiful, lovable, sexy, or kind. Tell yourself how proud you are of yourself. Whatever you say, say it with love and a generous heart. And reciprocate that love by receiving it with an open heart.

This is a moment to connect with the perfection of who you are while allowing yourself to feel your spirit And please know: you are your own best friend. You have your own back.

This ritual can be as long or as short as you like. You can say one sweet sentence or you can go on and on about how amazing, adorable, and precious you are for as long as you desire. The most important part is not the length of the ritual, but to receive the words graciously.

When you feel complete, take a moment to thank yourself, your loved ones on the other side, and your higher power for holding space for this self-love fest.

As you cultivate this new relationship with your body via your sensations, mirror work, self-pleasure, and sweet-talking, you will start to notice both subtle and big shifts. You'll notice that it starts to get easier to look at yourself in a loving way. You'll genuinely feel gratitude for certain parts of your body that you completely hated before. You'll notice that you're not saying as many judgmental things to yourself about your body. You'll notice that you'll want to look at yourself in the mirror more because it feels good to connect with yourself. You'll be enraptured by you and how sexy and sensual you are! Let the momentum take a hold of you and run with it.

You'll eventually get to a place where your limited definition of beauty that was dictated by society or your family is now expanding into a new definition, one that is coming from inside of you, from a feeling born in your body versus a false idea of perfection. You will find yourself living in a dream state, but it's based in reality. You don't have to live up to a false standard anymore. You can create your own standard that's based on your connection with the truths that live within you. They were just covered with shame, but once the shame releases, you will be able to identify those truths based on love that has been living inside of you since you were born.

We all were born with the knowledge that we are perfect as we are. We've just had layers upon layers of lies implanted in us. I love that gemstones are quite breathtaking, even when they're not perfect. Even the most beautiful diamond has imperfections, and that's what makes it uniquely perfect. Do you really want to look like someone else? We are not meant to be clones. We are human and we are special in our own ways and that not only includes our personalities but our appearances too. I want to encourage you to find the beauty in who you are. Own it. Get turned-on by it, really start to shine.

CHAPTER 10

Sleep, Food and Exercise... Oh my!

"Your body is a temple but only if you treat it as one."

— Astrid Alauda

As you've learned, spiritual bypassing causes backed-up emotions in the body which can lead to illness, pain, etc. But what happens when we emotionally bypass our physical needs? It's not talked about in the self-development community, but it's something I've personally experienced in the past, and I see many others doing the same. It's easy to use "doing the emotional or spiritual work" as an excuse to not do the physical work. When we ignore one or more of the realms, an imbalance is created. In some healing communities, there is a hierarchy, and the physical realm is on the bottom.

In my experience coming from a history of putting all of my attention on the emotional and spiritual and pretty much avoiding the mental and physical for most of my life, I can tell you that each realm is equal because they rely on each other and impact each other, just as yin and yang do. They have different qualities, unique to them, but each is just as important as the other.

Being healthy is the key here and as a result of being healthy, your body will become the appropriate size for you. This isn't about chasing a weight. It's about taking exquisite care of yourself in all ways, including your health. It's true what they say, that health is wealth. If you don't have your health, the most extreme result is that you will die. The other side is that you will have a low quality of life, of exhaustion, and no energy to create the life you desire. In a sense, you may feel like the walking dead because one day falls into the next and there's no sense of purpose or connection to yourself. Being healthy is the priority in this chapter. When you are healthy, you feel alive and are ready to take on the world and live with passion.

Cultivating Good Sleep Habits

I am starting with sleep because it's something that people have an idea of how important it is but don't prioritize it because they don't really know how important it is.

Quality sleep not only allows your body to recover and restore after a workout; it is a key ingredient in releasing weight but also heals every other aspect of you – emotional, mental, and physical. If you don't get quality sleep, your cortisol hormone can elevate which can cause weight gain, high blood pressure, muscle weakness, stress, etc.

Unrestful sleep has also been known to cause more sugar, carbohydrate, and caffeine cravings. If the body is exhausted, it needs something external to give it energy. But here is the thing, our energy should come from a healthy internal state that is sourced by healthy nutrients for the mind and body and a state of being. If it's not, it's a false sense of energy that covers up the root issues.

The interesting part that I have observed in my acupuncture practice is that stress is usually the cause of unrestful sleep. Most people tend to go to bed too late because they can't shut their minds off (stress) or they can't stop looking at screens, like TVs, computers, or phones (avoiding stress). Or they are eating or drinking too much alcohol too often or too late (numbing stress). Or they aren't moving their body (stress buildup). Or they have been drinking coffee all day because they're trying to hit a work deadline (stress).

Just because you get eight hours of sleep doesn't mean you are getting the quality sleep your mind and body need. Are you tossing and turning or waking up in the middle of the night? Do you wake up feeling tired? Do you need coffee or caffeine to get your day started? If so, then you're not getting quality sleep.

Here's some ways that you can get better sleep:

- Daily meditation.
- Consistent exercise.
- Go to bed by 11pm.
- More time in nature.
- Integrate a nighttime ritual (discussed in the next chapter).
- Check if your blood values are off and get the minerals and vitamins you need.
- Decrease sugar, carbs, caffeine and alcohol (especially in the late afternoon/evening).
- Do the entry point rituals.

Intuitive Eating

Intuitive eating is the remedy for emotional eating. When you emotionally eat, you have a clear indicator that you are off-balance somewhere and you're probably not fully listening to your inner wisdom, feelings, and sensations. It is important to build your intuitive muscles in this process. Doing so will serve you, not only with releasing weight, but in all areas of your life. This starts now with trusting what your body is telling you, day to day, moment by moment.

Food is necessary to maintain our life, literally. But we can also be alive but not living. I'm always amazed at how people are alive but never drink water and consume a large part of their meals as processed foods. If this is you, ask yourself if you really want a life where you feel energized, and if you do, are you ready to really live one?

I ask these questions because, when you feel revitalized, it feels like living on purpose. But, it's hard to feel this fully when you are unhealthy. Being healthy doesn't equal being skinny either, but it does mean that you are making conscious and informed decisions. Are you connected to your food? Do you know where your food is coming from? Do you look at the ingredients that you're ingesting? Get curious about what you are putting in your body and the chemical effects it has. It's quite fascinating actually. The human body is beyond miraculous, and we take it for granted most of the time.

My goal isn't to tell you exactly what to eat. I will make suggestions, but this path is not a diet. Everyone has a different constitution and preferences. When we put food into our bodies without being conscious and mindful, we can get into dangerous territory, especially when we have a history of emotional eating. I'm not saying to never eat sugar, carbs, etc. I would never say that! I am a foodie and will always have my fair share of pasta, fried chicken, and ice cream. But making conscious choices versus unconscious choices are two very different things.

This is where the practice of witnessing yourself comes into play. When it comes to food, staying present within yourself is the key.

Checking in and asking yourself radically honest questions will help you stay true to your desire of releasing weight and feeling good while doing it.

I found out during my weight-releasing journey that I wasn't as hungry as I always thought I was. Before I started paying attention, I was in a habitual cycle of eating all the time without awareness. I would just put things in my mouth without thinking about it. I didn't really connect with how and what I was eating or how foods made me physically feel because I was living with a baseline of feeling yucky to begin with. I didn't know that I could feel so good, energized, and strong in my body because I never gave myself the opportunity to experience anything like that.

Give yourself permission to experiment with listening to your body and following through with what it tells you. Play with asking yourself, "What would happen when I eat this? Or that?" Create a container to research what feels good and what doesn't. Learn when you're really hungry and when you're not, when you're eating because you're stressed or when you're bored. If you've been an emotional eater all your life, like me, it will take time and practice. But the key is to play with it. Be curious.

I recommend creating a food awareness section in your Self Journal (explained in the next chapter) as you get to know yourself better in these ways. This is not to track calories! I don't believe in that. More so, it's to create a higher level of awareness when it comes to food or any habits you're shifting. Write down all that you've observed in your research on a daily basis.

For example, this could be an entry: "I thought I was hungry this afternoon. I ended up eating some toast with butter. It wasn't satisfying at all. I still felt 'hungry' even though I wasn't really hungry. Now looking back, I realize I wasn't hungry in the first place. I was feeling lonely. I just wanted to feel connected to something or someone." The nugget here is that there's a new awareness of what hunger is and isn't. I now have a body memory of that moment, of when I thought I was hungry but really wasn't. I can use that memory anytime in the future when that similar feeling arises. This is redefining your conditioned habits around food, one experience at a time. With time and practice, you will create a "catalog" of these body memories that you can also tap into for guidance.

Mindful Eating Ritual

Before you eat, send loving energy to your food. Thank it for the nourishment it will provide you. Take a bite and chew. Pay attention to the taste and textures and chew more slowly. Enjoy every bite and savor it. You may want to put your utensil down in between every bit to bring more presence to the experience. Be aware of your emotional state. Do you have an urge to eat faster? Watch your thoughts. Is your mind drifting to you to do list or is it present with your experience of your meal? Take your time and let your level of hunger catch up with you naturally. But mostly importantly, enjoy the act of eating, of taking in nourishment and sustenance.

When you are finished eating, take a moment to thank your food, yourself, your loved ones on the other side, and your higher power for holding space for this deliciously mindful experience.

There are hunger hormones in our bloodstream that communicate with our brain and send a signal when we are hungry and full. The thing is that it takes about twenty minutes to receive the full signal. So if you're wolfing down food, you will most definitely overeat and feel stuffed. But the great news is that this is avoidable if you eat mindfully. Take your time, and give your internal body systems a chance to guide you. Plus, food tastes so much better when we take our time.

Most people who have struggled with overeating won't stop eating until they feel uncomfortably full. But again, it's been such a habit that it feels normal to be that full. Try experimenting with how it feels to eat until you feel satisfied. That means your stomach feels comfortable, and you don't feel hungry anymore. Ask yourself, "Am I wanting to continue eating because my body or my mind is telling me to?" Then wait for the answer. If you pause and give yourself the space and time to be present while both preparing and also while eating your meals, you will have a better chance of not overeating.

If you are craving something that is outside of the structure you have designed for yourself, ask yourself why. You may already be clear that you want to emotionally eat and if that's the case, take out your journal and start writing. Your prompt is: "I want to eat _______ because I am feeling _________." Let yourself feel the emotions that are there and question any beliefs that are showing up.

If you still want to eat the thing, then you have three options.

- Eat it and enjoy it with all of your being by releasing the guilt.
- Find another food that is comparable, but healthier (i.e. yogurt instead of ice cream) and notice if that does the trick. ▪ Reach

out and connect with someone because you may want to eat because what you're really needing instead is support and connection.

As a guideline, do not keep junk food in your home. Having easy access to foods that are not healthy for you will possibly tempt you in moments when you are feeling emotionally overwhelmed. This doesn't mean you can't ever eat them; it simply means that you are creating good boundaries with yourself to prevent sabotage.

Since the foundation of my teachings is based on yin and yang, it's important to allow flow (intuitive eating) and also create structure (intermittent fasting). Staying in tune with this balance will create a powerful and divine environment for you to powerfully shift your relationship with food and eating.

Intermittent Fasting

I'm such a geek when it comes to the body. I research, research, research! Then I practice on myself to see what feels good to me and use that information to learn more about myself and what I need.

In my extensive research, I've learned that every time you eat, your insulin spikes, even if you eat something super healthy like kale. If you are eating throughout the day, including snacking, your insulin will spike every time. This consistent spiking of insulin can cause your body to become insulin-resistant, and as a result, your body gains weight, especially in your stomach region. Learning this kind of blew my mind!

The other part that's important to acknowledge is that we currently live in a culture that eats way too much and way too often. We have been conditioned by society to put something into our mouths at all times because somewhere along the line there was a massive lie disseminated, which told hopeful weight-releasers and really everyone for that matter, that it's healthier to eat every two to three hours. Our culture has been cultivated to live in excess and overindulgence as a way to disconnect from what's happening underneath the surface. Feeling hunger has also been skewed into a thing that needs immediate attention or else we will die. No, folks, you will not die. Hunger is not an emergency.

You will learn what levels of hunger you really have because right now, you may only have two buttons: hungry and stuffed. There's quite a spectrum in between those two states, and intermittent fasting (IF) will help you discover the full range.

The way intermittent fasting works is that everyday you have a fasting period and an eating period. These can be in different ratios, but what has worked well for me is a daily sixteen-hour fasting period followed by an eight-hour eating period. You can choose the time of the day that works best for you. I prefer having my first meal around noon, my second meal around 4 p.m., and my last around 8 p.m.

I recommend starting with a twelve-hour period of fasting and a twelve-hour eating period. Over the course of a week or two, increase the fasting period to sixteen hours.

Since insulin spikes every time you eat, I recommend no snacking and eating meals every four hours. This means that you'll need to add more healthy fats in your diet; avocados, nuts, olive oil, and ghee are all great choices. Healthy fats help to sustain your hunger longer. I also recommend cutting your sugar and carbs down quite a bit because chemically they make you get hungrier faster and, more realistically, ravenous, which will make the four hours between meals torture. Believe me, I learned the hard way. Finally, it's important to drink a lot of water with electrolytes and eat plenty of veggies when you're doing IF.

For more information on intermittent fasting, watch Dr. Berg or Dr. Rhonda Patrick's YouTube videos.

When you create structure in your day for your meals, you are more apt to follow it versus saying, "Oh, I'll just wing it," and opt for takeout. So, create a plan of what you'll eat and when, but more importantly, be willing to listen to your body in the moment because she always knows best.

I have found that IF mixed with intuitive eating feels the best for me. It's the perfect balance of yin and yang. It will require you to practice tuning in to yourself within this new eating schedule. For example, I just shared with you my typical eating schedule, but that's not what I do every day. It's the structure I typically use, but there are days when I feel hungrier earlier, and so I'll have my first meal earlier. There are days when I want to eat more carbs, so I let myself eat more carbs. There are days that I only want one or two meals a day. There are other days that I have a pint of ice cream. I don't believe in being too rigid because that typically creates resentment and frustration, which can lead to sabotage, emotional eating, ultimately binging and giving up.

I fully own and celebrate how much I love food, and I will never make myself eat in a rigid way. I also know that when I create a structure that works for me, I feel so much better. Allow days or meals where you can eat things outside of your healthier meals. This will be different for everyone. For me, I loved planning what I was going to eat during my weekdays. I made those meals really healthy, and I let myself eat more treats on the weekends. You need to get to know yourself and what your flow is. Then, you can play around with different structures to see what works for you. But within whatever structure you decide on, it's important to be kind to yourself. This isn't about being militant or overly rigid. It's about developing a more intimate relationship with yourself so you can hear your body more clearly and trust what she's telling you.

Side note: I don't call those weekend meals "cheat meals" because I'm not cheating on anything. I'm just living my life in a conscious way that feels good to me.

Truthfully, sometimes I'll fall off the horsey, and find myself in an old pattern of emotionally eating. I don't beat myself up for this because I have realistic expectations and know there will be bumps in the road. It's about the practice of doing my best, being kind to myself, exploring the emotional and mental aspects that need tending to and loving up on my body, and then choosing to recommit to the process. Then repeat!

This is a journey, people! Not a destination. I know you've heard it many times and you get it, but are you practicing it?

So, my recommendation is this: Create an intermittent fasting schedule, follow your body's innate wisdom, and you are well on your way to feeling alive in your body! In my own experience of doing IF, I experienced a huge increase in energy, easy weight release, better sleep, a clearer mind, a better mood, and a higher level of connection with my body. Now let's move onto to exercise!

Exercise

The thing that I dreaded doing all my life has become something I

crave now. I am still pinching myself when I think about how much I enjoy working out and have a relatively easy time to motivate myself to do it. Coming from a history of being sedentary, I can safely reassure you that this is possible for you too! I hate to admit it, but I was a couch potato when I was at home, and I am a homebody. I felt so heavy, physically and energetically, that I wouldn't do much of anything. I had no motivation whatsoever.

But then during this particular transformative year, after the breakup and doing all of the forgiveness work, belief work, intuitive eating, and intermittent fasting, my body started screaming for me to exercise.

I was walking my dog, Ceba, in the park one day. At that time, she was sixteen years old and still spunky. She would get these bursts of energy and just start running, and of course, like the good dog mom that I am, I would run with her.

But on this particular day, I felt and heard my body telling me in no uncertain terms: "You need to start jogging!" It was clear as day, and I made the decision at that moment. I would start jogging, something that I had always said I hated, and would never do. Jogging in particular was something I would judge others for doing when it was cold out, saying, "Those people are crazy."

It was fall at this time, and starting to get chilly, but I was determined because I could not ignore the desire my body had so clearly expressed. So I started jogging at the park. I didn't want people to see me jog because I felt uncomfortable, and like a fraud. I felt embarrassed because I knew I was going to be slow. But I was committed.

I started out by greeting the park when I entered. Hello, trees! Hello birdies! Hello, sky! Hello, lake! Hello, earth! Hello, air! Thank you all so much for being here and holding me. Remember, I was going through a break-up at this time, so I also needed to connect with the healing aspect of nature as well. Nature symbolized trusting the divine energy that was surrounding me.

As I would try to motivate myself to start jogging, I heard my mind say things like, "I don't want to jog," "There's no way I'm going to get around the lake," "I don't feel like doing this," "I'm tired," and numerous other sabotaging thoughts.

So I focused my mind and came up with other thoughts that felt better and truer. "You just have to run for short spurts," "You can always take a break when you get tired," "You're just starting, and it's going to take time to build this jogging muscle," "You got this!"

So I just started jogging, and trust me when I tell you, it was hard. I could only jog for a minute at a time before losing my breath, but I timed my walking break and started jogging again when the alarm went off.

Eventually, on my first day, I made it around the lake! I took too many breaks to count, but I did it. That was a huge accomplishment for me, and I celebrated!

I decided I wanted to jog three times a week. I set up my goals and did the work to get my butt to the park. Over time and with a lot of patience and the right mindset, I started to pick up my speed and could run longer durations without stopping. I was amazed by how fast my body was getting conditioned and I was so proud of myself for showing up. Eventually I was able to run around the entire park (3.35 miles) stopping only two or three times! I decided to get even more inspiration by signing up for a 5k race with my friend who is an experienced runner, and we started training together once a week.

She taught me more about body alignment and sprinting in order to condition my lungs and to improve my time. Thanks to her tips, I was able to run around the park without stopping, and the 'killer' hill didn't 'kill' me anymore! It was a powerful experience to give myself a chance at winning by trusting the process and knowing that it was going to take time, practice, and lots of self-compassion for me to reach my goal of running a ten-minute mile. I never hit that goal at the race – it was around 10:30 – but I started at a twelve-minute mile, and that was huge. Getting around the park without stopping was huge, and it still is.

Let yourself take in how good it feels to take care of yourself. The pride you feel when you make a choice that you may not have made in the past. If you don't feel motivated to exercise, get yourself turned-on first. Do a dance break, put on a cute workout outfit, pump yourself up with mirror work.

If you are still having a challenging time getting yourself to exercise, I suggest connecting with a buddy and doing fun things like Zumba classes, speed walking in the park, yoga, trampolining, or going out to dance or salsa class. This is all about meeting yourself where you are and finding the pleasure in it. You will create momentum as you go, as

I did with jogging, so start somewhere that feels doable for you with the intention of increasing your intensity and quantity.

Exercise Mirror Work Ritual

If you have access to a mirror, put it in front of your workout station at home or look at yourself in the mirror at the gym. Look at yourself as if you are your own trainer, cheering and coaching yourself through the workout the entire time. Look in your eyes and tell yourself how amazing you are and how you're killing it. Visualize yourself as the athlete you are or whatever you desire to be and believe it.

See yourself as your future self now. See yourself as whatever you desire to be now. If your desire is to feel alive and energized, you can visualize yourself with the glow oozing out of you already. See it in your minds eye. If you desire to run a 5k, visualize yourself running that race. If you desire to feel sexy walking down the street, visualize that. Look straight into your eyes and soul and see yourself as that person. Drop right into that vision. Let your vision fuel your exercise and let the intensity of the exercise fuel your vision.

This future self is who you are now. She's inside of you already; she just hasn't come out on the physical level yet. She's in the energetic desire realm. But that doesn't make her less real.

When you are finished exercising, take a moment to thank yourself, your loved ones on the other side, and your higher power for holding space for this alchemical journey.

Fear Burning Ritual

As you begin to sweat as you intensify your exercise, imagine the fear, shame, and any emotion that has been living in your body armor being burned out as you exercise. This is an alchemical process that requires you to use your focus, your imagination, and your cultivated ability to feel.

Feel and visualize the emotions being released out of your fat, your cells, your being, as you increase your heart rate and sweat. You are moving the stuck energies that have been residing inside of your system, releasing the emotional weight that has been holding you down. Let the intensity of the exercise fuel your focus and let your focus fuel your intensity.

When you are finished exercising, take a moment to thank yourself, your loved ones on the other side, and your higher power for holding space for this alchemical journey.

Not living in your potential is the thing that makes you feel depleted, stuck, and tired. That includes our physical potential. Your energy (yang) needs to be used by movement. Your blood (yin) needs to be nourished by food. Your entire self needs quality sleep to integrate. When you don't honor this foundational truth, you don't give yourself the opportunity to live your best life. It blocks your channels to the source energy, which includes creativity, love, financial abundance, and intimacy in relationships. It takes a certain level of courage to listen, trust, and act accordingly. The question is if you're willing to do things differently.

CHAPTER 11

Adulting 101

"Awareness without action is like sitting in a poopy diaper."

— Unknown

I always prided myself on being a free bird and doing what I wanted, when I wanted. That's partly why I've worked for myself for almost twenty years. I needed freedom and to be fluid. But here's the thing: I found out that I actually crave fluidity and structure. I noticed that when I have structure, I not only follow through more, but I experience more flow. The structure provides the freedom to flow. You will find that as you create a clear container for yourself, you will feel more at ease and more inspired to take action.

Structure and discipline are considered dirty words in some healing communities. Everyone is so focused on being connected to the yin that they tend to disregard the yang. As you are well aware of by this point, I honor and respect both energies, and I am clear that they both need to exist in our process as equals, and in tandem with each other. The internal yin work is just as important as the external yang work. The yin flow is just as important as the yang structure.

Goal Setting

Goal setting is a powerful tool. It sets you up for success by aligning you to your desire, while having a plan so you can take massive action in whatever ways make the most sense for you. Goal setting empowers you to go for it! It supports you in staying accountable to yourself.

Goals are like that nagging best friend that won't let you off the hook when you tell them your biggest dream.

Goal Setting was the tool I needed to get myself into shape – literally and figuratively. To be able to see on paper what it was that I envisioned for myself and the steps I needed to get there. It was a potent reality check, and one that I needed, welcomed, but also rolled my eyes at in the moments I wanted to give up. But thank goddess for this tool because I honestly don't know if I would've been able to follow through without putting my goals on paper and returning back to work with them every single day.

When I began my weight releasing journey, I got clear on what it was that I desired for myself, my big 'why?', and the actions that needed to be taken to get there. Here's the except from my first goal setting process:

Big goal: Shed my body armor, specifically 20 pounds in 13 weeks.

My why: Because I want to experience the feeling of confidence from having completed something that historically has been challenging for me.

Progress goals:

1. Release 1.5 pounds per week
2. Jog 12 minutes per mile
3. Go to bed by midnight

Actions:
For Progress Goal #1

- Intermittent fasting

- Eat out once a week max Cut
- out ice cream

For Progress Goal #2

- Jog 3x/ week around the park
- Jogging sprints 1x/ week Trampoline
- 2x/ week

For Progress Goal #3

- Start night-time ritual after walking Ceba Stop
- screens at 10 p.m.
- Listen to Yoga Nidra meditation every night in bed

As I continued this process, and got to know myself better, I made various adjustments to the actions. It was a true time of discovery. I learned that I could depend on myself in this new physical form; that my word to myself was full of integrity; and when I was unable to rise to the occasion, I practiced being kind to myself. And choose to start fresh again.

Goal Setting Ritual

- Begin by writing out all of the desires you have for your body for at least 10 minutes. Don't overthink it. Just let yourself do a brain dump. Write everything that you desire no matter how confronting or silly it might feel. Let yourself feel the release of moving all of that energy from your brain to the paper.

- Now review all of the desires you listed and pick the top three desires.
- From those three, pick the number one top priority.
- Write out what measurable goal can happen in the next 13 weeks. Make it as specific as possible. For example: releasing 1.5 pounds a week or jogging a twelve-minute mile.
- Then write down all of the actions you need to take to reach that goal. Brain dump here again.
- Pick the top three actions that feel the most impactful and realistic for you in this moment.
- Schedule those actions in your calendar and incorporate them into your life.
- Continue to check in with your goals and actions every day to keep you inspired and motivated.

Now if you're a geek like me and love checking off boxes and like having a tool to keep you organized and accountable, you have to check out the Self Journal tool! www.bestself.co

Congratulations! You are now on your way to building new healthy habits.

Creating Habits

You've lived a certain way for most or all of your life, and now you're trying to do this completely differently. It can feel overwhelming if you see it that way or you can see it as creating shifts one day at a time. Something to keep in mind is that resistance creates self-sabotage. It's important to be aware of the common ways people are likely to halt their progress:

- Future-tripping about failing.
- Overdoing it by implementing too many new habits at once.
- Thinking that something else needs to be finished before beginning.
- Thinking that a resource is needed before beginning. For example: a gym membership, money, etc.
- Thinking that their body is broken and unable to exercise.

You'll know when you're sabotaging because you'll feel stuck and yucky. Being able to be radically honest with yourself, and call yourself out when you get glimmers of sabotage, will change the game because it actually feels good to have integrity with yourself.

I also find that it is necessary to redefine what self-care actually is. True self-care is not over indulgence. My client described it best: if a child were acting out, would you give them a cupcake? I'm thinking probably not! The same is true with you. Do you tell yourself that laying around all day in the house is being gentle with yourself when what you are really doing is avoiding and over- indulging? This is not to say that laying around the house is bad and should never happen. I'm pointing to a specific moment when you're in resistance, and instead of doing your best you choose to not do anything. I find that many women who are trying to release weight tend to conflate indulgence with being gentle. Indulgence is not being in tune with where you are in the moment, as it dishonors your needs and desires. Authentic gentleness asks that you be in tune with your needs and desires, while at the same time not letting yourself off the hook by letting resistance win.

When creating new habits, I recommend pairing each new habit with an existing habit. Here's some examples:

- You already make tea every morning but now you put your supplements next to the tea to trigger your memory.
- You already put lotion on your body after taking a shower but now you pair it with mirror work and self-pleasure rituals in the morning.
- You already brush your teeth at night but now you pair it with shutting down your screens right after you brush your teeth.

Habit Pairing Ritual

- Take out a pen and paper and draw a vertical line down the middle of the paper.
- On the left side, make a list of the healthy habits you currently have ingrained in your day to day living.
- On the right side, make a list of the habits you desire to integrate in your life.
- Scan both lists and see if there are any habits that can be paired together that makes sense as seen in examples above.
- There is no need to do this for all of the habits listed. It's just a starting point of building new habits and a positive mindset around habits in general.

It's important to take it one step at a time and at your own pace. Don't try to make all the changes at once. Pick the thing that feels most accessible to you and stick with it. The more you stick with it, the more your confidence grows. And then you'll feel like you can do the next thing. You are creating your mindset every time you follow through with something that you didn't know you could do. Creating new habits is a mind game and about building momentum. So be strategic and smart about it. This is the time to use your intelligence!

The whole process of changing your lifestyle is the perfect research study to get to know yourself. So while you are practicing with your food, exercise, and sleep and other self-care routines, you are learning about yourself. This is not about only getting to the goal, but also about diagnosing and discovering along the way. You will learn about what works for you and what doesn't. And then you will adjust based on what you've learned. It's all research! That's life.

If you're feeling stuck and unmotivated, the best thing to do is shake it up a bit. Do something different than what you're currently doing. Move your body. Not necessarily exercise but move your body to get your breathing up as a way to change your state of mind. Jump up and down. Take deep intense breaths. Take a walk outside. Take a shower. Just do something different.

Also, those moments are a good time to reset your intentions. Get really honest with yourself and ask yourself what your intention is for the next hour or so. This will keep you from spinning out into the future. One step at a time. Procrastination and feeling stuck happen when you're living in the future or ruminating on the past. So if you just focus on the moment and what you want to do in the immediate future, you will find that you are naturally building momentum.

Momentum is where it's at and that's why it's crucial for me to create a morning and night time ritual. Every time we go to sleep, our momentum stops. So in the morning, it's time to get the momentum going again. If I don't have a ritual to help me get my mind and body flowing, it will make the rest of the day more challenging and with more resistance. When I create my morning ritual, I make sure to pick a couple of things that will help me to create the right state of mind. A nighttime ritual is just as important because coming down pleasurably from the day means that your sleep will be more restorative, which means you are setting yourself up to have more energy and clarity for the following day.

Creating a Morning and Nighttime Ritual

Here's a list practices for the morning and evening. Pick two for the morning and two for the night.

Morning practices:

- Meditation
- Write in your journal
- Stretch or yoga
- Take a walk outside and connect with nature
- Dance break
- Mirror work
- Listening or reading something inspirational

Nighttime practices:

- Shut down screens two hours before sleep
- Write in your journal
- Stretch or yoga
- Take an Epsom salt bath with lavender essential oil
- Read a book
- Self-pleasure
- Listen to a guided sleep meditation

Digesting Your Body Changes

Digesting the changes that are happening to your body is as important as the actions taken to release the weight. Have you met people that released a bunch of weight but never felt comfortable in their new skin, so they unconsciously gained it all back? Or perhaps that was you at some point. Taking the weight back happens when the internal and external aspects of you are not in resonance. What I mean by this is that the inside has not caught up with the outside and a state of tangible, ongoing embodiment has not yet been reached. This is why I stress the importance of doing the internal work while we build a sustainable connection with our bodies along the way.

So do your mirror work and look at yourself with amazement about the shifts you have made, big and small. Look at all of you and see yourself with your love filters. See how beautiful you really are.

I personally love before and after photos, and I highly recommend them as a way to digest your body's transformation. Take a photo of your whole body from the front, back, and side angle and continue to take photos once a month. Then create side-by side-photos before and after photos with a photo editor for the front, side, and back angles. Then check yourself out and see all the small or big changes you've made in that time frame compared to the last photo. This is not an exercise to scrutinize yourself. This is an exercise to celebrate your wins!

Start to release your clothes that don't fit. As you release the weight, buy new clothes that express who you are at this point in your life. This will not only support you in digesting your new body, but you'll also feel this latent desire to own your sensual and sexual self and radiate your light. When a woman is able to own and embody their unique sensual nature, magic happens! When a woman owns her sensuality, she owns her power and light.

Community

Practicing in a community is always beneficial. Not only will it add to your accountability, but it will also provide support when you are not feeling so hot. To be witnessed on your journey in a safe space is a transformative experience, especially when it comes to something so personal and protected as the fear fat suit. Allow yourself to be vulnerable and share what's happening for you: share your emotions, your well-earned wins, and definitely your failures, disappointments, and bumps on the road. Also, through witnessing other people on their journeys you can be reminded that you are not alone, that your problems are not unique. Finally, you'll be inspired to keep going. It's a win-win!

The Other Side

CHAPTER 12

Flow

"Life is a series of natural and spontaneous changes. Don't resist them - that only creates sorrow. Let reality be reality. Let things flow naturally forward in whatever way they like."

— Lao Tzu

You have now walked through the yin and yang portals. You have completed many rituals, meditations, and exercises. I'm proud of you and I hope you feel proud too! I'm imagining that you're discovering all kinds of things about yourself. You're recovering old memories, getting reacquainted with your inner child and all the gifts and dreams you once had. You're feeling a lot more connected to your body, releasing stories that no longer serve you and having breakthrough after breakthrough. This has been a process of you practicing trusting yourself to hold space for you. And now you are expanding your capacity to be even more present and receptive by bringing flow into your everyday life.

Yay! Now what?

Now you stir it all in a pot and mix it up! Mix all the practices up and allow yourself to experiment by combining the emotional, mental, and physical rituals together along with everything else you've learned. You are exploring and experimenting in both new and wondrous ways that are unique to your personal flow. Experiment with listening to your internal guiding system and have fun with it. Continue to play with all of the elements you have been introduced to. Make it a game.

Have you ever watched a surfer catching waves? That's flow. They are having the time of their life while being so attuned to nature and what each moment is being asked of them. Being able to ride the energetic yin and yang waves will allow you to be in harmony with the same flow states as that surfer. When you tap into this mysterious, invisible, energetic realm, you open yourself up to living at one with source energy.

In Chinese medicine, if there's no flow it means that stagnant energy and/or disease are present. In order to unblock the stuck energy and create movement in our lives, we need to connect with this unseen world and learn how to be with it. And that's exactly what you've been cultivating while doing the practices in this book. You are increasing your ability to feel, be present, and connect to your body, mind, and spirit. These new found skills will support you in harnessing the energetic connections that will unite you with your flow.

To be in flow requires:

- Presence: Being present to feel, hear, or see the intuitive whispers and 'knowings' that arise in you.
- Trust: Trust those 'knowings'.
- Action: Follow through with what those whispers are telling you.

Flow is one hundred percent about being present with the reality of this moment. When you release your attachments to your expectations and your ways of trying to control life, flow automatically happens. You don't have to work to be in flow. The energy is moving with or without you, but if you choose to flow, you will find that your quality of life will increase exponentially. When you are gripping onto fear and trying to manipulate situations to be the way you want them to be, you have taken yourself out of flow. You know when you are flowing when life feels fluid, clear, and like it's happening organically, with ease, and you're exactly where you are supposed to be. This happens not only with "positive" situations, but is also true with painful ones. You can grieve and still be in flow. As a matter of fact, if you practice feeling your emotions, you will eventually be able to feel how good it feels to move through your pain while in flow.

Benefits of Flow

Experiencing greater intuition is the ultimate confirmation of your alignment in all the realms. You feel a sense of freedom because you are moving through life with a deep knowing that you are being guided, moment to moment, that living from a place of trusting your internal guiding system actually feels more secure than trying your old ways of grasping for security by attempting to control the outcome.

Can you imagine how good it would feel to do this with your body care? Trusting that you will know when to eat, what to eat, and when to stop eating; trusting that you will listen to your body's wisdom to get up and exercise or rest in the ways your body is craving; trusting that you can just check in and know where you are at this moment; trusting that you can get back into flow when you fall out of it.

When you trust the flow, you are connected to your truth. You trust what you're feeling so when you feel a truth arise in you, you trust that too. And being in tune with flow, you are able to speak that truth.

There's such a cultivated connection with source energy that your clarity is grounded in you. There is no more questioning why you are here and what your purpose is because you know who you are. There's a sense of uprightness that takes over your body and energy, a satisfaction within yourself and living from what you know to be true.

When you trust the flow, you also trust yourself and the process. Women who have been hiding behind their weight and have tried to release it by only attempting to change their diet and exercise have lost their trust in the process and in themselves. When in flow, you know that you are doing your best and that your word holds power and integrity. You also are so much more loving to yourself and know that when you say you are going to do something that feels in alignment with what you desire, you do it and you surrender to the steps it takes to get there because you know that you can do whatever it is you put your mind to.

When you trust the organic flow of life, you naturally open up your receptivity. Most people move through life in defense mode, with one or more forms of shields. When you allow yourself to surrender to what is arising in you in every moment, you shed the protective barriers that prevent you from receiving love, your desires, attention, financial abundance, connection to self, and anything else. There's a feeling of openness and relaxation because you know that you are worthy of receiving all of the abundance you desire. There's a graciousness and ease that washes over you because there's no more fighting to get what you want.

Looking back on my life, I recall having so much abundance, whether it was loving support from friends, financial success, or supportive parents. But I was never satisfied because I wasn't allowing myself to receive any of the goodness coming my way. I always felt it was never enough, but that was just a reflection of what I thought about myself. I created many layers of "stay away" without even knowing it. But once I started to do the work of loving myself, through the entry points, I was able to receive all of the love around me and in me.

When people talk about receiving, usually they are referring to objects associated with cultural definitions of wealth and success: cars, jobs, relationships, and money, but as you start to build your receiving muscles, you will find that the most precious gift is a new ability to receive love, not only from other people but most importantly from yourself and the Universe, receiving it because there's a new and expanded level of trust in you that you no longer need to defend.

Being connected to your flow is another way of saying that you are at one with source energy. It means that you have no doubt about your connection to the divine and all of the abundance it provides. It means that you are surrendered to the miraculous unfolding of your life and know that the Universe has your back. You no longer question what it means to feel connected to the energy that connects all living and nonliving beings.

CHAPTER 13

You Are Your Own Artwork

"Our deepest fear is not that we are inadequate. Our deepest fear is that we are powerful beyond measure. It is our Light, not our Darkness, that most frightens us."

– Marianne Williamson

I believe our purpose in life is to radiate our own unique light in the world. This process of releasing weight is not only about shedding fat – it's about shedding the protective barriers that hide our light because at one point or another in your life, you took on a belief that it's not safe to be a radiant glowing goddess.

When I fell in love with my body and released my fear fat suit, I had this moment while walking to the train station. I was feeling like a million bucks, and I heard a whisper in my mind that said, "You are your own artwork." This is what I mean by radiance is purpose. You can work in any field, even if it doesn't feel like your true calling, but still feel connected to who you truly are. You are already living your purpose when you are glowing from the inside out.

Here's the secret: when you are radiating like this, you will be divinely guided to the work that is your calling.

It's the owning and honoring of who you are that allows you to be a shining star, shining so bright that you inspire everyone who is in your presence. Whether you say something or not doesn't matter. They will feel you oozing with light and that light is love and can cause the most powerful ripple effects. So even if you're in a "dead-end job," you will be creating ripples of love. This is how I believe we can change the world, one person at a time.

When you own this truth, you can embody it. Let that truth sink into how you move, walk, talk, exercise, eat, work, make love. You can make a choice to let what has shifted on the inside (self-love) come out to express itself on the outside.

What I noticed a couple of months into my journey was that I started to walk differently, partly because my body was changing and becoming more physically aligned and partly because I was feeling so good on the inside. One day, I caught myself walking down the street, and I felt like I was gliding. I was upright, and my head was held high. I had a pep in my step, and my hips were swaying from side to side.

I used to be the type of person who didn't want attention. I mean I did, but I didn't. I didn't feel safe, so I did my typical invisibility cloak thing by not making eye contact and by dressing myself down. I had a challenging time receiving attention, and when I got attention, I would shut down internally by either pretending to be confident like I wasn't fazed by the attention or just going small. But when you radiate, you feel safe in your body, with yourself, and with others. You feel safe everywhere!

Own Your Glow Ritual

I invite you to feel the yumminess of your body when you're walking down the street. Feel your body. Feel the alignment in your spirit. Feel the alignment of your spine. Open your chest and your heart. Connect with your muscles while moving. Feel your hips swing. Feel energy and electricity moving through your body. Make eye contact with strangers. Perhaps give them a little smile or a shimmery eye twinkle. Offer them the gift of seeing the beauty of love that lives within you. You are an embodied goddess. There's no need to hide it anymore.

CHAPTER 14

Conclusion

"The journey of a thousand miles begins with one step."

— Lao Tzu

I wrote this book because I have experienced the power of shedding my fear fat suit and how that has completely changed my life in every way, shape, and form. I now know how it feels to be truly alive and living a life on purpose after a lifetime of suffering. My intention in writing this book is to inspire you and others to choose the path of self-realization.

I wrote this book for the little girl in me that was scared and hiding, and for the little girl in you that wants to be seen and share her highest version of herself into the world. It's such a gift for me to be able to share this with you, as it has created deeper healing for myself. My hope is that this book will have a ripple effect and continue to create deeper healing for you and the world.

I believe we all have a light burning bright within us already, but we just need to shed the layers that are hiding it. These security blankets are creating a false sense of safety. When I felt the elation and love arise in me while releasing my physical and emotional weight, I saw the real me for the first time.

I was able to own exactly who I am with no more shame, invisibility cloaks, or body armor. I was able to let people see the deepest and most true parts of me that always wanted to be seen. I became more generous with my heart, with strangers, friends, and family because I no longer was in survival mode. I touched my biggest desire of being able to love another human unconditionally for the first time because I fell in love with myself.

I became a woman of true faith, and even in the course of losing one loved one after another, I was able to stay connected to my knowledge of what is true.

With all of this bursting out of me, I could not keep it to myself. It had to be shared for others to receive. It has been quite an adventure for me to translate my internal process into something as concrete as words, and now coming to the end of it, it feels quite surreal. We have covered so much territory, and I am so honored that you have made it all the way to the end.

As you transform yourself, you will transform your life, and a natural outcome of that is you will feel inspired to pay it forward. That can happen with a smile to a stranger or sharing your story. Whatever it is that calls to you, I urge you to listen and do it. This life moves fast if we are not present, and we have the ability to slow down to choose connection to self and to others. Shine your unique light which is the highest level of expression of you, And in return, receive all the abundance that is magnetized to you.

This is the beauty of this life-changing journey: When you are connected to source energy you will never be able to withhold your light anymore. Take this process into your life and wrap your arms around it, embrace it. Live in the rituals and keep coming back to the practice every day. If you need reminders or inspiration along the way, revisit chapters that are calling out to you, call a friend on the path, or contact me for support.

You have opened the door to this brave new world, and it's time to step through. Don't turn back. Keep walking toward that light that already lives within you and be generous in sharing the gifts you hold.

Our personal transformations are a reflection of society's transformation. The more we heal ourselves, the more humanity heals. Be a direct warrior of change by doing the work on yourself first and foremost. The world needs it.

"You must be the change you wish to see in the world."

— Mahatma Gandhi

www.ingramcontent.com/pod-product-compliance
Lightning Source LLC
LaVergne TN
LVHW091318150826
845673LV00006B/1691